VIRGINIAN RAILWAY
In Color

William G. McClure, III & Jeremy F. Plant

Published by
Morning Sun Books, Inc.
9 Pheasant Lane
Scotch Plains, NJ 07076
Printed in Korea

Library of Congress
Catalog Card No. 2004106386

First Printing
ISBN 1-58248-142-3

To access our full library _In Color_
visit us at
www.morningsunbooks.com

ROBERT J. YANOSEY, President

DEDICATED TO
D. Wallace Johnson, August Thieme and the late H. Reid
Three childhood pals whose extensive and evocative photography of the Pocahontas Roads during the 1940s and 1950s has inspired generations of railroad fans.

ACKNOWLEDGEMENTS

Without the photographic work of many people a project like this would never be possible, but we first want to acknowledge the vision and drive of Bob Yanosey to set aside material on The Virginian Railway as he searched out slides for his many Morning Sun books projects. The Virginian disappeared into the Norfolk & Western Railway in 1959 and it was not widely photographed in color in any event, for a number of reasons. Bob knew he had the nucleus of a book; he then trusted us to try to put it together, for which we thank him.

We are photographers, railroad photographers, who appreciate fine photographic work. We also have a keen appreciation for the time, effort, and talent it takes to produce images that other people will want to view, over and over again. This volume presents such work. We are so pleased to be able to present the photography of Arthur Angstadt; Steve Bogen; Harry Bundy; Casey Cavanaugh; Robert Clarkson; Robert F. Collins; George Dimond; William Echternacht; William Ellis; F. V. Ewell; Steve Gibson; S. Goodrick; Matthew J. Herson, Jr.; Lawson Hill; Eugene L. Huddleston; D. Wallace Johnson; Bill McClellan; Russell F. Munroe; Homer Newlon; John Pickett; H. Reid; Kurt Reisweber; James P. Shuman; Richard J. Solomon; John P. Stith; August Thieme; William Volkmer; Roger Whitt; Aubrey Wiley; J. W. Swanberg; and Robert J. Yanosey. We further express our appreciation to the following for loaning us material from their collections: Bob Liljestrand, owner of Bob's Photo; the Don Ball Collection; Kurt Reisweber; Robert J. Yanosey; the Boston and Hawk Mountain Chapters of the National Railway Historical Society; and D. Wallace Johnson. A special thanks to Chuck McIntyre of Richmond, Virginia, for making available to us the work of the late H. Reid and the late Jack Stith, and to Brian Solomon for sharing the works of his father.

Finally, we express our gratitude to the members of the Norfolk & Western Historical Society, lead with great skill and dedication by James Gillum, for the efforts of the Society in preserving in its Archives an extensive collection of VGN drawings and other materials, and for allowing us the use of some of that material herein, which is credited to "N&WHS Archives".

LEFT, PAGE 1 & DUST JACKET •
A pair of the Virginian's last new locomotives, twelve 3300-horsepower ignitron-rectifier units delivered by General Electric in 1956, rest at Princeton, West Virginia, on July 29, 1958, 16 months before the railroad disappeared into the Norfolk & Western. (Richard Jay Solomon)

My Granddad sold coal; on the road each week for Old Ben Coal Company. Knowing my interest in trains, he frequently returned with gifts for me, the kinds of things routinely handed out by the railroads to customers in those days: calendars and playing cards from the Chesapeake & Ohio; prints of N&W steam along New River; etc. One day in 1957 or '58 he brought me a little booklet that would ultimately lead me to this volume. I suppose I had heard of The Virginian Railway, but if so it had never made an impression on me; "Coal On The Move" changed that. The cover image of black and yellow Fairbanks-Morse Train Masters hooked me and began a lifelong interest in Henry Huttleston Rogers' grand adventure. With that introduction I pored over the back issue listing for *Trains* magazine and acquired copies with articles on the Virginian by H. Reid, August Thieme, and others.

After moving back to Richmond in 1974 I came to know, and have great affection for the "tres amigos" of the Pocahontas Roads: Wally Johnson, Thieme, and Reid. More than their photographs, which speak for themselves, over the years I have enjoyed the tales of their travels together through western Virginia and West Virginia in the 1940s and '50s. No Interstates, no motels, no fast food…bad roads, "flathead" Fords, rooming houses, and roadhouses. Shooting film during the day and developing it in the bathrooms at night; being chased out of town by locals after getting too friendly with somebody's girl in a roadhouse. Looking down both barrels of a moonshiner's Parker on Great Flat Top Mountain! There is a book there waiting to be written, but that's for another day. For now, we are pleased to dedicate this volume to them for the many ways their photography of the Pocahontas Roads has inspired us and for their generosity in sharing it with all of us in so many ways.

For a railfan of the period it must have been easy to overlook the Virginian. It passed through rugged and remote country and it was overshadowed by its two larger rivals, the C&O and N&W, which were never too far away. As a consequence, finding photographs of and other information about the railroad has been a challenge for its fans for years. Only through the dogged persistence of individuals has information been tracked down and then shared generally. I would like to recognize the efforts, in no particular order, of Lloyd Lewis, Kurt Reisweber, Aubrey Wiley, Tom Salmon, Bob Moore, Roger Nutting, Marty Swartz and Tom Dixon of TLC Publishing, to name just a few, for keeping the flame alive and in making information about the Virginian available to the public in many ways.

This is a book of color railroad photography, and not a history of the railroad. We sincerely hope that some day the definitive history will be written, perhaps by Lloyd Lewis. For now, we are pleased to be able to present the best of the color slides available to us. The geographic coverage will be incomplete; there are few photographs of the many coal branches, and there is almost no coverage of the Fourth Subdivision from Mullens to Deepwater and the line from Elmore to Gilbert. If there is unpublished color material from those areas, we sincerely hope publication of this volume will stimulate its publication. Having said that, we think the reader will still find a few gems herein! And it's another great story of personal ambition and drive in the building of the industrialized America of the 20th Century.

Bill McClure
Richmond, Virginia

Like many others of my generation, my first exposure to the Virginian came through H. Reid's inspired 1961 book. It was one of the few railroad books in my college library, and captured the railroad, its people and its setting in a way that moved me deeply. I relocated to Virginia in 1967, too late to see the real Virginian before it was absorbed by its big and ambitious neighbor, the Norfolk & Western. But trips to Virginian country, especially in the New River region and into the hills of southern West Virginia to Princeton, Mullens, Oak Hill, and Page, helped me understand the appeal of the VGN. In the early 1970s, the former VGN lines were the best places to find the remaining Train Masters, and often the big six-axle Alco Centuries (some of them riding on the trucks of trade-in FMs). I grew friendly with some of the N&W employees at Elmore, most of whom had a background on the old Virginian and were happy to talk about "the old days." Chasing the last run of the Train Masters from Roanoke to Elmore and back in 1973 really brought home how ambitious Henry Rogers and Colonel Page had been to push an ultra-modern, highly efficient railroad through the wilderness of the West Virginia mountains.

The Virginian was a challenge to photographers. It was far from most major urban areas, hard to follow by good roads in most places, and overshadowed in density by the Norfolk & Western. Ironically, I suspect many VGN color shots exist today because of the immense appeal of the N&W right next door, still operating steam through the 1950s; it was easy enough to steal some time to visit the VGN and record a few shots of it as well. Certainly, the traction and electric fans had good reason to make shooting the VGN a high priority; it was in many respects the Eastern equivalent of the Milwaukee's Pacific Coast Extension, operating big electrics over high trestles in forested mountains far from civilization (although Western juice fans may find the looks of the big streamlined units more reminiscent of the Great Northern's post-World War II units employed in the Cascades). Many shots in this book reflect the dedication to electrics of James P. Shuman and Sanford Goodrick, hard-core electric fans who knew where to go to find electric power and had the photographic skills to record them brilliantly.

Starting this project, Bob, Bill and I wondered if we would find enough shots to make this book a complete look at the Virginian. We were surprised to find so many good shots out there, and so many fine photographers viewing the VGN through their artistic perspective. I'm indebted to Bill McClure for his vast knowledge of the Virginian; it's truly his labor of love. We hope you enjoy the look at one of the truly unique railroads ever constructed in America, the Virginian Railway.

Jeremy F. Plant
Hershey, Pennsylvania

COAL ON THE MOVE

VIA THE VIRGINIAN RAILWAY

The wild and beautiful state of West Virginia has been blessed over the years, some might also say cursed in some ways, by an abundance of two great natural resources: immense quantities of high-grade bituminous, or "soft" coal and dense hardwood forests of oaks, walnut and, for a time, elm. The coal was, and remains a part of a belt stretching from western Pennsylvania to the southwest through West Virginia, western Virginia, eastern Kentucky, Tennessee, and into northern Alabama. For reasons that perhaps only a geologist could explain, the highest-quality coal (measured, among other things, by BTU content and unburned byproducts, i.e. smoke!) was formed eons ago under western Virginia and southern West Virginia. Whether by coincidence or by design of nature, that formation occurred under some of the most rugged, dense and beautiful terrain in the country, the Appalachian Plateau. Unlike the pine forests to the east and south, the Appalachian Range, which itself stretches from New York state southwesterly to northwest Georgia and Alabama, produced great stands of hardwood trees, nowhere more remote and inaccessible than in West Virginia and western Virginia. It was timber and coal that brought "outsiders" to the wild country, men with dreams of riches; some with dreams and riches!

In 1873 a geologist named Capt. Isaiah Welch confirmed what long had been suspected, that great deposits of recoverable coal were in the vicinity of Flat Top Mountain in southern West Virginia and western Virginia. A 13-foot thick seam was found on the surface of a farm near what is now Pocahontas, Virginia. It wasn't long before the N&W began a 75-mile extension from its main line at Radford, Virginia, down New River to Glen Lyn, then into West Virginia and up the valley of East River. It climbed up a steep grade to reach what is now Bluefield, West Virginia, highest point on the N&W, before dropping down to the Bluestone River. The extension ended a short ways up Laurel Creek where the new mining community of Pocahontas was built. The story is told that the wife of N&W Vice President, Frederick Kimball, named the town after the Indian Princess of early Colonial times. In any event, the first car of "Pocahontas" coal was shipped in 1883, and from those times forward the name "Pocahontas" has been synonymous with one or more seams of extremely high-grade bituminous coal, and with the three railroads that hauled it east and west. Matoaka, a town on both the Virginian and the N&W, is another name for Pocahontas. The N&W would go on to continue its New River Extension west along the Tug Fork of the Big Sandy and the Big Sandy itself to reach the Ohio River and beyond.

The C&O had taken a different route in an attempt to reach both the coal fields of West Virginia and the commerce along the mighty Ohio River. It crossed the mountains of western Virginia from a base at Clifton Forge and dropped into the valley of the Greenbrier River, which it followed for a distance to reach New River at Hinton, some distance north of the N&W. It then followed first New River and then the Kanawha to Huntington, West Virginia, on the Ohio, which was reached in 1873. The C&O would send numerous branches up the valleys on either side of its main line, and sometimes up and over ridges, to reach scores of mines developed over the years. For many years the C&O was the largest originator of coal in the country, the majority of which would come from the West Virginia fields it tapped.

Lying between the N&W to the south and the C&O to the north was a rugged, largely inaccessible plateau that was known to contain large quantities of recoverable coal... recoverable to be sure, but valuable only if you had a way to get it out and to market. Like the fields tapped by the N&W, it was part of the so-called "Smokeless Coal Fields," with stores of bituminous coal that had low volatility; that is, they had smaller amounts of volatile matter that produced smoke and pollution. Such coal rivaled anthracite coal for use in home heating, and was much in demand for maritime use, at a time before diesel propulsion for vessels when coal was the fuel of choice. This region was still a wilderness as late as the turn of the 20th century. As the demand for high-quality coal grew, so did the value of tapping such a rich source of fuel. Such situations seem to always attract dreamers, schemers, visionaries…and sometimes, moneyed men. This was the case with the Smokeless Coal Field and the birth of the Virginian Railway idea.

Col. William N. Page of Ansted, West Virginia, a town high above New River at the end of a short, steep C&O branch, had made a small fortune in the mining business as a civil engineer. He had also learned something of the railroad business by helping convert the original narrow gauge line into Ansted to standard gauge. Page had met one Henry Huttleston Rogers, an eastern businessman of considerable accomplishment and wealth, and sometime after 1896 had discussed with Rogers an idea to purchase a narrow gauge railroad extending from a connection with the C&O at Deepwater, at the mouth of Loup Creek on the south bank of New River, up Loup Creek to a sawmill at Robson, a distance of four miles. Had Page's vision ended at Robson it seems doubtful that Rogers would have been interested. But instead of just enjoying the fruits of his extremely successful career, Page had studied; he had studied maps, mining reports and surveys, including a survey of the 25,000 acre Wilson tract up Loup Creek. Since about 1871 it had been known that coal was on that tract, and it was coal that brought Page and Rogers to a plan: buy a railroad from Deepwater to Robson, then extend it about seventy-five miles south to a connection with the N&W at the town of Matoaka (pronounced ma-TOE-ka). Coal from the Loup Creek area could then be shipped either north to the C&O or south to the N&W, an arrangement Rogers assumed would produce rate competition. With that plan, Rogers threw his considerable intellect, experience and wealth behind the plan. On January 25, 1898, the Deepwater Railway was incorporated in West Virginia to build a rail line 60 miles up Lower Loup Creek to Glenjean on Upper Loup Creek.

Rogers was born in Fairhaven, Massachusetts, in 1840. By the end of the century he was an extremely successful and wealthy businessman, an expert in oil development and refining who became a part of the Rockefellers' Standard Oil Trust as Chairman of its Manufacturing Committee, a trustee and a Vice President. He had amassed holdings in oil, gas, copper, steel, and banking. Now he was to be in the railroad business! By 1909 the Page plan would become The Virginian Railway and Rogers would have spent $40 million of his own money building it. There are few railroads that would carry the imprint of a single man to the extent that the Virginian would reflect Henry Huttleston Rogers. But we are getting ahead of ourselves.

As Page built the railroad, Rogers discovered that he could not get favorable rates from either the N&W or the C&O because the two had conspired to fix rates for this interloper. It is not clear whether C&O or N&W could have done anything to stop the construction of the railroad before it got started. If they could have, they let the opportunities pass and then had to suffer the consequences for half a century. Both Page and Rogers were formidable men, and after the C&O/N&W rate agreement, they determined to take the line all the way to Tidewater Virginia. By 1902 the Deepwater charter was amended to extend its rights to the Virginia state line, and in 1904 the Tidewater Railway was chartered in Virginia by Rogers to build west to the West Virginia line. There was a plan afoot, but by the time anyone could connect the dots, the deed would be done! While Rogers put up the money, he largely stayed in the background and let Page build the two railroads. The Tidewater began laying rails west from a crossing of the Seaboard Air Line at Algren on the outer edge of the Great Dismal Swamp. As the Deepwater built south and approached Jenny Gap, a pass into the valley of the Guyandot River, they were discovered by C&O survey crews hard at the same task. It took fist fights…and no doubt gunfire…before a decision of the West Virginia Supreme Court permitted the Deepwater to exercise eminent domain to secure a right-of-way across the lands of the C&O and its subsidiaries through Jenny Gap and beyond.

In 1907 the name of the Tidewater was changed to The Virginian Railway and the Virginian acquired the Deepwater. That same year the road acquired 611 acres of land at Sewells Point on the Elizabeth River in Norfolk, adjacent to the land of the 1907 Jamestown Exposition, for a yard and coal piers. In 1909, after 11 years of hard work, the last spike connecting the two lines was driven just west of the bridge over New River at Glen Lyn, Virginia, and the first of two coal piers was opened for business at Sewells Point. Not only was the vision of Page and Rogers achieved, it was achieved in spectacular fashion. Both men had engineering backgrounds. Perhaps because of those backgrounds, or perhaps because they had uncommon foresight, their new road was constructed to the highest standards of the day; wide clearances, big bridges, rights-of-way wide enough for two tracks and heavy 131/132 pound rail. Because the road was among the last major lines constructed, it was built with the latest in standards and equipment for cuts and fills, bridges and tunnels. While the main lines and branches in West Virginia had to contend with steep grades, once they reached Roanoke, Virginia, the route to Tidewater was essentially downhill.

In April 1909 Rogers made an inspection trip over his new railroad from Norfolk to Deepwater; he could not persuade his aged friend Mark Twain, who had come to Norfolk with him on his yacht, to venture out to the wilds of southern West Virginia with him on his private car. On the way out Rogers was ebullient about the prospects of the new road, and even imagined it extending west to the Great Lakes. However, he died two weeks after finishing his tours, and his heirs never shared his grandiose dreams. The Virginian was destined to remain what it was at his death, a conveyor belt for coal to move from the Smokeless Fields to Tidewater.

The 60-mile line from Deepwater to the major coal assembly yard at Elmore, just south of Mullens, had, and still has, a roller coaster profile. Eight miles south of Deepwater at the top of a steep grade, the road established a yard and town named Page after the Colonel. Page became an assembly point for coal on the north end of the line. (The Deepwater-Elmore line became the Fourth Subdivision of the New River Division. The Third Sub extended from Elmore to Roanoke. The Third and Fourth Sub comprised the New River Division, better known as the "West End".) Page had a 100' turntable and a large rectangular engine house. It was a base for mine runs and trains to the C&O connection at Deepwater, and later to the New York Central across the Kanawha River after a bridge was built in 1931. From Page the line east (south) climbed a 10-mile 2.02% grade to Silver Gap. A mile from Silver Gap, at Oak Hill Junction, the White Oak Branch extended into the hills on very steep grades to reach mine tipples at Carlisle and Lochgelly

The main line descended from Silver Gap on a 1.1% grade, then ascended 8 miles of 1.75% to the summit at Harper; only to descend again and then up 9 miles of 1.65% to Jenny Gap, where the VGN and C&O survey parties had fought. Exiting a tunnel at Jenny Gap the line descended 15 miles of 1.65% to Elmore. At Gulf Junction, 2 miles north of Elmore at Mullens, the 35-mile long Winding Gulf Branch headed northeast into rich coal lands southeast of Beckley. At Elmore the Guyandot River Branch extended 53 miles west to a connection with both the N&W and the C&O at Gilbert. Coal off the "Gulf" and from the Guyandot would become the backbone of the Virginian's earnings for decades.

We will cover the details of the remainder of the road to Tidewater later in this volume and focus now on a brief overview of operations. The Virginian was a simple railroad to understand. At one time it operated four scheduled "time freights", nos. 71/72 and 73/74, between Norfolk and Deepwater and locals on both the West End and East End. It also operated both through passenger trains between Norfolk and Charleston, West Virginia, and a number of locals to service the coal branches. By the time period covered in this volume, the years 1950-1959, the road was down to two time freights (71/72), two through passenger trains (3/4), and locals in each direction on alternate days. It was coal that paid the bills and dividends to the shareholders and it moved in large quantities to the piers at Sewells Point, with a much smaller amount heading west to the NYC interchange. From Elmore Yard several times a day a "Hill Run" would take 3000-4000 tons of coal to Clarks Gap on Great Flat Top Mountain, up 10 miles of 2.07% grade with 12 degree curves and five tunnels. The Hill Run would set off the cars at the top and a later Hill Run would be filled out with enough cars for an 8,000-10,000 ton train for the run to Roanoke and on to Sewells Point. The operation was simple; its execution was a challenge.

To move the tonnage the VGN began with 2-8-2s and 2-6-6-0s and then experimented with a 2-8-8-2. For pusher service on Clarks Gap it had Baldwin build an enormous, one-of-a-kind triplex with a 2-8-8-8-4 wheel arrangement, the last set of drivers being under the tender. The engine used steam faster than the boiler could produce it and for that and other reasons,

it was a complete failure. In 1918 the road had ten massive 2-10-10-2s built for the same task. They would prove to be extremely powerful…and very slow; anything over a fast walk's pace was speeding for the huge engines, the only ones of their wheel arrangement ever employed in the U. S. They served for many years in both road and pusher service. Beginning in 1919 the VGN assembled a roster of 38 compound 2-8-8-2s of USRA design that was the backbone of service in the coal fields and on the main

line from Roanoke to Norfolk until replaced by diesels. Passenger trains were originally handled by 4-4-0s, then 4-6-0s and finally six elegant 4-6-2s that hauled the trains until passenger service was discontinued in 1956. The last steam acquired, in the 1940s, moved the road from a "drag era" philosophy into the realm of "Superpower": eight huge 2-6-6-6s and five 2-8-4s of C&O design and fifteen 0-8-0s purchased second-hand from the C&O. They had relatively short lives as steam goes; the road dieselized between 1954-56 with two models from Fairbanks-Morse and one second-hand Alco/GE 44-ton switcher.

There were many things that made the Virginian unique, such as massive steam engines, big coal gondolas, big bridges and trestles, etc. The feature that seemed to attract the most attention from fans was the 133-mile long electrified zone between Mullens and Roanoke. The conversion to 11,000 volt overhead power occurred in 1925-26 to alleviate operating problems on Clarks Gap grade. Once again, the VGN pioneered very powerful electric motors in three waves: three-unit boxcab, jackshaft motors from Westinghouse in 1925-26; four huge two-unit motor-generator sets from General Electric in 1948; and twelve 3300-horsepower ignitron-rectifier units from GE in 1956. The electric operation proved to be extremely successful and continued until June 30, 1962, two years and seven months after the acquisition of the VGN by the N&W.

Sometimes overlooked in the history of the VGN is the impact it had on Southside Virginia, the region between the mountains and its Tidewater terminal at Sewells Point. Southside Virginia, that area east of Roanoke and north of the North Carolina border, was a largely agricultural region relatively untouched by industrialization or urbanization. The VGN pushed its tracks east from Roanoke to Norfolk without much concern for generating traffic along the mileage in the Old Dominion, and passed through no large cities along the way. The area still remains sparsely populated and definitely "off the beaten track," or at least major highways. The VGN had to build from scratch a town to serve as division point on the long stretch east of Roanoke. It acquired land in Lunenberg County, halfway between Roanoke and Tidewater, and created the town of Victoria, named for Queen Victoria.

The final chapter of this brief overview of VGN history is the disappearance of the Virginian into the N&W. It may be hard to believe today after several decades of restructuring of the American railroad system through one merger after another, but the acquisition of the Virginian by the N&W on December 1, 1959, was the first acquisition by merger of two independent lines in decades, and two parallel lines to boot. The railroad industry had been heavily regulated for decades by the Interstate Commerce Commission, which, among many functions, had to approve all railroad combinations or acquisitions of control, etc. The ICC had never looked with favor on combinations of parallel lines since in theory, they lessened competition. The ICC approval of the N&W-VGN proposal was a watershed event that set the stage for a wave of parallel mergers to follow beginning in the 1960s, some of which were successful (e.g. Atlantic Coast Line-Seaboard Air Line), and some of which would prove to be disastrous (e.g. Pennsylvania-New York Central). In any event, after three attempts over four decades, the N&W was finally successful in eliminating a competitor, tapping new coal originations, and restructuring its traffic flow to Tidewater.

The post-merger changes, some subtle, some not, came quickly. VGN engines were renumbered by adding 100, save for the 6, the Alco/GE 44-ton switcher, which was retired. Within a month the remaining steam locomotives on the property were sold for scrap, as were the remaining Squareheads. On the West End Train Masters began to take coal trains east to Roanoke under the wires. Trains were lengthened, necessitating a third unit, whether a Train Master or one of the 1956-built EL-Cs. Only the big 1948 General Electric EL-2Bs operated as before, but even so one set was broken up and a single unit was based at Whitethorne as a helper for the now heavier eastbound coal trains. The operating plan was, and remains to send tonnage east over the former VGN line to avoid the steep climb out of Roanoke over Blue Ridge on the N&W, and to send merchandise and empty hoppers west over the N&W. Connecting tracks were installed at Kellysville, West Virginia, just west of Glen Lyn, and at Salem, Virginia, so that trains off the VGN could follow the N&W line to Roanoke, avoiding the grade to Merrimac on the VGN, and then go back to VGN rails to enter Roanoke. Other than these changes, for quite some time after the merger the operating pattern of the former VGN lines on the West End remained essentially unchanged. Over time, though, nearly all of the many coal mines served by the former VGN branches were closed for one reason or another. By the end of June 1962 the Electrified Zone was history!

On the East End the VGN trackage was, and still is, used east of Roanoke to Abilene, where it joins the N&W main to Norfolk. Eventually, the remaining VGN main line to Norfolk was removed, and Sewells Point was sold to the U.S. Navy for expansion of the Norfolk Naval Operating Base. The FM units assigned to the East End were moved to yard service at Lamberts Point and N&W power ruled east of Roanoke. For more detail about the state of operations on the former VGN lines after the merger and into the era of Norfolk Southern, we refer the reader to Kurt Reisweber's well–crafted *Virginian Rails*.

As a postscript, a curious reader might wonder how ownership of the VGN passed down from Rogers to the N&W in 1959, given that Rogers died in 1909. After his death the railroad was owned by his heirs until it was acquired by the famed Mellon family of Pittsburgh in 1937. The corporate vehicle the Mellons used to acquire the railroad was Eastern Gas & Fuel Associates, a subsidiary of the Koppers United Company, a company controlled by the family. EG&F owned extensive coal properties in the area served by the Virginian and was also the largest shipper of coal from

Tidewater to northeastern markets via its Mystic Steamship Company subsidiary. Thus, EG&F assured itself reliable transportation and no doubt favorable rates and car supply, in spite of ICC regulation. Since the railroad was so controlled, it never had a public relations department, and until the mid-1950s its Annual Reports to its shareholders were very plain, fact-filled documents without any hint of "fluff" or public relations content. That began to change in the mid-1950s, at about the same time a group of minority shareholders in EG&F began seeking ways to squeeze more value out of EG&F. One way was to realize the inherent value in the Virginian via a merger with N&W. That interest of the minority shareholders intersected with the long-held desire of N&W to acquire the VGN, and it came to pass. Characteristically for the Virginian, in his last Annual Report, President Frank D. Beale addressed the proposed N&W merger, which would bring an end to his corporation, with all of four sentences.

Fans of the Virginian lament its passage; it was one of those rare railroads that really was like a family and was very friendly to enthusiasts. Realistically, though, something would have happened sooner or later. The VGN was so dependent on coal traffic that it had few options if its traditional commodity flow changed. There were 52 mines served by the Virginian at the end of 1958. but only a handful are operating on former VGN lines today. Many of the coal branches have been abandoned. Enough of that, let's now look back at it during its peak years in the 1950s.

RIGHT • *The cover of the first Virginian Annual Report was plain, in keeping with both the style of the era, and with the utilitarian approach that would guide the railroad its entire life.*
(N&WHS Archives)

FOLLOWING PAGE, RIGHT • *Until the mid-1950s Virginian Annual Reports were rather dull documents, filled with impressive information and data but without ornamentation. Until 1954 the only color to be found was this system map found in several Annual Reports from the 1940s, in this case from 1947. While the East End was a relatively straight shot across Southside Virginia, the map's designers substantially improved the profile of the West End!* (N&WHS Archives)

VIRGINIAN STEAM ROSTER

Class	Type	Quantity	Number Series	Date Built	Builder
SA	0-8-0	5	1-5	1909/10	Richmond/Baldwin
SB	0-8-0	15	240-254	1942/43	Lima
PA	4-6-2	6	210-215	1920	Richmond
MB	2-8-2	42	420-461	1909/10	Baldwin
MC	2-8-2	18	462-479	1912	Baldwin
MCA	2-8-2	5	480-484	1912	Baldwin
BA	2-8-4	5	505-509	1946	Lima
USA	2-8-8-2	20	701-720	1919	Richmond
USB	2-8-8-2	15	721-735	1923	Richmond
USE	2-8-8-2	7	736-742	1919	Alco
AE	2-10-10-2	10	800-809	1918	Alco
AG	2-6-6-6	8	900-907	1945	Lima

VIRGINIAN ELECTRIC ROSTER

Class	Type	Quantity	Number Series	Date Built	Builder
EL-3A	1-D-1	12	100-111	1925/26	Alco/Westinghouse
EL-1A	1-D-1	6	110-115	1926	Alco/Westinghouse
EL-2B	B-B+B-B	4	125-128	1948	General Electric
EL-C	C-C	12	130-141	1956	General Electric

VIRGINIAN DIESEL-ELECTRIC ROSTER

Class	Type	Quantity	Number Series	Date Built	Builder
DE-SA	B-B/44-tonner	1	6	1941	Alco-GE
DE-S	B-B/H16-44	40	10-49	1954-1957	Fairbanks-Morse
DE-RS	C-C/Train Master	25	50-74	1954-1957	Fairbanks-Morse

1910

First Annual Report

The Virginian Railway Company

For the Fiscal Year Ending June 30, 1910

The Virginian was built for just one reason: to make money by hauling high-grade West Virginia bituminous coal from Wyoming, Raleigh, Fayette, Mingo and Mercer Counties to the Port of Hampton Roads, Virginia, one of the world's great natural deepwater harbors. From there coal would be shipped to Europe and to the Northeastern states in coastal shipping. Hampton Roads is the point at which the Elizabeth, Nansemond and James rivers and the Chesapeake Bay come together and merge with the Atlantic Ocean. The Chesapeake & Ohio Railway followed the James River down the Peninsula of Virginia, between the James and York rivers, and built its great ocean terminus at Newport News on the north side of Hampton Roads. On the south side the Elizabeth River flowed north and formed the boundary between the cities of Portsmouth and Norfolk. The river has three branches which shape the landscape and posed obstacles to the building of railroads into the area.

The Norfolk & Western reached the south side of Hampton Roads in 1858. In 1885 it built its first coal pier at Lamberts Point in Norfolk, on the eastern bank of the Elizabeth River across from the city of Portsmouth, where both the Atlantic Coast Line and the Seaboard Air Line built terminals. As the last railroad to arrive in the area, in 1907, the Virginian had to cross all of those lines and also find a spot for its own terminal. It chose a 611-acre site near the mouth of the Elizabeth River, north of the N&W and adjacent to the U. S. Navy's Norfolk Operating Base. In 1909 it constructed its first coal loading pier, Pier 1, followed by its second and last in 1925, the New Pier or Pier 2. The yard at Sewells Point grew to 85 miles of track holding some 6500 cars, nearly all of which were coal cars at any point in time. It also had an adjacent ground storage facility it constructed, but which was operated by Eastern Gas & Fuel Associates, a subsidiary of Koppers United Company, Virginian's controlling shareholder from 1937 until the N&W merger. The peak year for Sewells Point was 1956, when 10 million tons of "black gold" was loaded.

After N&W acquired the Virginian in 1959, the piers at Sewells Point were taken out of service and were eventually sold to the Navy for expansion of the Naval Operating Base. The yard was used for coal storage until the mid-1970s when the land was sold to the Navy.

On August 11, 1956, while riding a C&O ferry from Newport News to Norfolk, noted steam era photographer August Thieme photographed Piers 1 and 2 from the Elizabeth River looking southeast. The engineering challenge all such loading facilities had to solve was how to efficiently move large quantities of dense coal from ground level into the holds of ships of varying lengths and configurations. It had to move up, out and back down. Virginian's piers originally used what the road called the "high loading" method wherein coal was dumped into electrically powered conveyor cars, which then ran out the piers and dumped their loads into ships via telescoping chutes. It was a complicated electrical and mechanical system. *(A. Thieme)*

ABOVE • This photo of Pier 1 gives a great view of the complexity of the operation carried out thousands of times a day. Two coal cars at a time would be pushed up the ramp in the foreground by a "barney" or "mule" between the tracks onto a tilting table beneath the shed–like structure. The cars were tilted and their cargoes dumped into a pan, which were hoisted to pier level where the coal was dumped into a conveyor car. The electrically powered conveyor car would travel out the pier and dump its load into a chute extended out into the hold of a collier. Pier 1 conveyor cars held 60 tons and Pier 2 cars held 110 or 130 tons. In the late 1950s Pier 2 was modernized with a low-level rotary dumper that fed conveyor belts that carried the coal up for dumping, eliminating the conveyor car operation. *(F. V. Ewell)*

ABOVE • In May 1959 conveyor car 20 of Class CV-3 was at Princeton, out of service but in excellent condition. The car was built for use on Pier 2 by The Alliance Machine Co. of Alliance, Ohio, in 1924 as one of four with a 130 ton capacity. It was the last such car purchased. The cars operated by electricity taken from an overhead trolley wire by a small trolley pole which sat on the overhang at the other end of this car. *(Roger F. Whitt)*

RIGHT • In 1957 Virginian took delivery of its sole tug-boat, the *W. R. Coe*, named for the Chairman of the road's Executive Committee at the time, and seen here on the cover of the 1957 Annual Report. The 105 foot long, 1500 horsepower vessel was used to move ships around Piers 1 and 2 for the last two years of Virginian's existence. *(N&WHS Archives)*

BELOW • In 1959 the N&W renamed the *W. R. Coe* the *R. B. Claytor* and transferred it to a subsidiary, Coal Terminal Towing, which then contracted out tug services at Lamberts Point to Curtis Bay Towing. In this photo from 1978 we see the *W. R. Coe* gliding through Hampton Roads in its N&W incarnation, prior to being sold in 1983 to Boston Fuel Transportation of Massachusetts. *(Steve Gibson)*

LEFT • Switching chores at the port terminal were carried out by 0-8-0s in steam days and by 1600 horsepower Class DE-S Fairbanks-Morse H16-44 road switchers in the last years. In 1909 Alco's Richmond Works delivered three 0-8-0s in Class SA, numbered 1-3, and in 1910 Baldwin delivered two more to the same specifications, numbered 4 and 5. They had 51" drivers, were relatively light and had small, sloped-back tenders that carried 10 tons of coal and 5000 gallons of water. Nos. 1, 3 and 5 were scrapped in 1933 and 2 in 1955. No. 4 was given to the City of Princeton, West Virginia, in 1957 and subsequently was sold to the Virginia Transportation Museum in Roanoke, where it remains the only preserved Virginian steam locomotive. On May 2, 1954 the 4 was resting at Sewells Point. *(A. Thieme)*

ABOVE and LEFT • On November 6, 1954 SB Class 0-8-0 242 was drilling coal cars at Sewells Point. The 15 members of the SB Class were built in 1942-43 by Lima for the C&O. By 1950 the C&O no longer needed as many steam switchers as EMD and Alco delivered increasing numbers of diesel switchers. Its 30 youngest (1948) 0-8-0s were sold to N&W and the next 15 youngest were acquired by Virginian for a very low price. They could be found in the yards at Norfolk, Victoria, Roanoke, Elmore and Princeton. By January 1955 the new H16-44s were working the yard and #242 was stored. She was the first of her class to be scrapped, in January 1957. The bold lettering was the signature of Virginian equipment throughout its existence. Not once did the road adopt an "economy" paint scheme of any kind for anything!

(Two photos, Russell F. Munroe, Jr.)

ABOVE • SB Class 250 was resting at Sewells Point on March 7, 1954, with a rusting MB in the background. The fifteen SBs were built for the C&O by Lima in 1942-43 and purchased by the VGN in September 1950. After the War the C&O had begun purchasing diesel switchers and found itself with nearly new 0-8-0s that were excess. It put a number up for sale in 1950 and the N&W purchased the thirty built by Baldwin in 1948; the VGN took the next youngest group. The entire class was scrapped between 1957 and 1959. *(A. Thieme)*

BELOW • On shore leave during his tour of duty with the Navy, Russ Munroe found SA #2 with sister 4 behind it at Sewells Point on November 6, 1954, five months after being displaced at Suffolk by an Alco/GE 44-ton diesel, the 6. The 2 was the last member of Virginian's first order for three engines in 1909; it was scrapped in 1955.

(Russell F. Munroe, Jr.)

ABOVE • A broadside view of the 242 out of service shows the chunky lines of the SBs, with snow on the ground at Sewells Point in January 1955. *(H. Reid)*

ABOVE • Fairbanks-Morse H16-44, road Class DE-S, 29 appears to be drifting down from the crest of the hump at Sewells Point on October 9, 1956. The yard had a receiving and classification yard, a "barney" yard and a yard for empty coal cars exiting the piers. Coal cars were pushed over the hump into the barney yard, from whence they would be pushed into the unloading mechanisms. The H16s were used in both road and switching service on the East End. In a radical departure from its Pocahontas Road contemporaries, N&W and C&O, Virginian adopted a flashy, high visibility black and yellow paint scheme, and its diesel power was kept relatively clean by coal hauling standards. *(William Echternacht, NRHS collection)*

"The 1909 MB was the best thing that happened to the Virginian since Henry Huttleston Rogers. Without the MB chapter, the Virginian story might have concluded long before it did." - H. Reid, 1961

In his classic 1961 work, *The Virginian Railway*, which remains the best single volume on the history of the road, H. Reid made no secret of his affection for the 42 members of Class MB, nos. 420-461. Reid analyzed, through the eyes of an historian but with the gifts of a journalist, why an engine of ordinary size, with no extraordinary design features, no breakthrough technology, and nothing special in any way could be considered "great". If anything so complicated can be summarized, it would be that the engines did everything that needed to be done – switching, coal drags, time freights, and troop and passenger trains – from 1909 until the end of steam. In 1954 8 of the 42 were still on the roster and the last steamer to operate on the East End was MB 432 in 1956. They were versatile and reliable; as they were bumped from mainline duties they proved to be as useful in local and switching services all over the railroad. For a road that operated an enormous 2-8-8-8-4 Triplex, huge 2-10-10-2s, and Superpower 2-8-4s and 2-6-6-6s, and pioneered in electric traction, that a 1909 2-8-2 would be considered its greatest engine is remarkable.

LEFT • On May 18, 1954 the cylinder cocks of MB 453 are open as it rests at Sewells Point. The MBs were built with square cabs and single air pumps. All but one, 430, would receive smaller, sloped front cabs and all would be fitted with dual cross-compound air pumps. Cab sashes were a red-orange shade and running board edges were painted aluminum. Roundhouse forces at different locations would often put their own touches to the engines, such as the aluminum driver centers on 453, or boilers wiped to a shine with fish oil. 453 was retired on March 31, 1955. *(John Pickett)*

ABOVE • MB 459 rested quietly at Sewells Point on March 7, 1954. 459 was one of the few MBs that were fitted with Duplex stokers; otherwise the class was hand fired. The Virginian steam class system was based on the common name of the type, the <u>M</u>ikado, with a letter denoting the series in alphabetical order. Thus, Class MB represented the second group of Mikados purchased by the road. 459 was retired on December 31, 1954 and was one of the last two MBs (with 432) scrapped in 1959. *(A. Thieme)*

RIGHT • MB 448 was drilling boxcars at Sewells Point on August 15, 1953. *(Russell F. Munroe, Jr.)*

ABOVE • Sister MB 446 sits out of service at Sewells Point on November 6, 1954, looking as if she has not turned a wheel in quite some time. She was not retired until March 31, 1956. In addition to the MBs, the Mikado fleet included 6 Class MAs built in 1905-07, 18 Class MCs built by Baldwin in 1912 and one member of Class MD, no. 410 built by Baldwin in 1921 from the rear engine of the ill-fated Triplex. Five members of Class MC were rebuilt and upgraded by the Princeton Shops in 1937-41 and were reclassified as Class MCA. So while the road had 66 Mikados, it was the 42 MBs that provided the bulk of the muscle. *(Russell F. Munroe, Jr.)*

ABOVE • On July 18, 1956 Jim Shuman captured MB 453 underway at an unrecorded location with a type of spark arrestor applied to a number of MBs that worked in urban switching. *(James P. Shuman)*

ABOVE • Class engine 420 sits under steam in Princeton, West Virginia on September 5, 1954. MBs originally carried road pilots, but as they were downgraded to switching and local services, they were equipped with footboards, and some had black and white safe-

ty stripes on the pilot. Most also had spark arrestors of some type, especially those in urban areas. Note the difference in the spark arrestor on 420 and those seen in the prior views of MBs on the East End. *(Homer T. Newlon, collection of D. Wallace Johnson)*

ABOVE • On the day after Christmas 1954 SB 250 was being coaled at Sewells Point. The facility was similar to the one in Roanoke. Coal was dumped from hoppers to a pan that was hoisted up and dropped into the tender. The layout was compact and served the relatively light needs of the Virginian well. *(H. Reid)*

BELOW • On Christmas Eve 1954 MB 459 was steaming quietly at Sewells Point with its August 1910 Baldwin builder's plate glistening in the sun.

(H. Reid)

ABOVE • H. Reid loved the human element of railroading and worked to record railroaders doing their work-a-day tasks. On Christmas Eve 1954, he framed AG 903 receiving attention with the working end of MB 447 on the left and the Sewells Point coaling station on the right. *(H. Reid)*

BELOW • SB 250 and MC 462 were being serviced at Sewells Point on November 6, 1954. The fireman of 250 is filling the sand dome and it appears the engineer is talking with one of the engine terminal workers. *(Russell F. Munroe, Jr.)*

In an era when railroad photography was dominated by "rods-down" roster shots and three-quarter "wedgies" for action, the late H. Reid (called "H" or "Reid" by his friends) and a few others were breaking new ground by experimenting with the traditional tools of photography, light, line, form and composition, to create arresting images more in the nature of "editorial" photography, rather than documentary. Reid was a journalist by trade and a story-teller at heart. His cameras became instruments to tell a story or to lead a viewer to find new insights into the familiar. No one loved Virginian steam locomotives more than Reid, and we are honored to present this tribute to his photographic skills and his love of Virginian steam with these examples of his art.

ABOVE • Reid dropped down to rail level to capture lovely PA 214 and train in Norfolk in January 1955. *(H. Reid)*

RIGHT • On a rainy, overcast day at Sewells Point in September 1956, a day when most photographers would have packed it in and gone home, Reid recorded MB 432, one of the last two MBs to operate, in this moody scene. The Kodachrome of the day was rated at an ASA of 10, making color shots like this a test of the photographer's skill and imagination. *(H. Reid)*

RIGHT • On a 35mm half-frame image, Reid recorded BA 2-8-4 506 at Sewells Point in April 1953.
   (H. Reid, collection of A. Thieme)

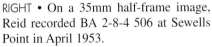

ABOVE • The 430 was the only MB to retain its original square cab; the other 41 were rebuilt with a slanted front cab that became the VGN standard. At the end of its service life it was still used in over-the-road duties on locals so it still carried a road pilot and did not have the spark arrestor screen applied to MBs used in urban areas. It was under steam on Christmas Eve 1954 at Sewells Point. The 430 was scrapped in March 1955. *(H. Reid)*

ABOVE • The MC Class had a balanced, powerful look about them. The 476 was resting between time freights at Sewells Point in June 1952. She was scrapped in June 1955. *(H. Reid, collection of A. Thieme)*

THE

VIRGINIAN
RAILWAY
.COMPANY

NORFOLK DIVISION

TIME TABLE No.

EFFECTIVE 12:01 A. M.
SUNDAY, MAY 20, 1956

EASTERN STANDARD TIME

VIRGINIAN RY.

For the government and information
of employees; not for the public.

J. P. STRICKLAND
Superintendent

B. MILLS
Asst. General Manager

D. C. KING
Vice President and General Manager

ABOVE and BELOW • Virginian's mileage was measured from Norfolk Terminal Station, which was ten miles by rail south of Sewells Point. Leaving Sewells Point Virginian trains traveled east then turned southeast for several miles before turning due south. Almost two miles from Sewells Point was Quartermaster Junction, Q. M. Junction in the timetable. In 1918 large piers were built at Tanner Point, just below Sewells Point on the Elizabeth River, for the transportation of Army troops overseas. A rail line was built to the site from a connection with the Virginian at what became Quartermaster Junction, so named because the piers had been constructed by the Army's Quartermaster Corps. The site became the Norfolk Army Base and saw much activity during both world wars. Over time the site became Norfolk International Terminals, a major container shipping facility now operated by the Virginia Ports Authority. On May 2, 1954 BA Class 2-8-4 #509 ripped through Q. M. Junction with empty coal cars, trailed by one of the road's modern steel cabs. *(Two photos, A. Thieme)*

LEFT • The cover of Virginian employee's Time Table No. 23 of May 20, 1956 for the Norfolk Division, the "East End". *(N&WHS Archives)*

Six miles south of Q. M. Junction the Virginian crossed the Norfolk Southern Railway, the original NS that ran from Norfolk to Raleigh and Charlotte, North Carolina. The NS operated two lines in the Norfolk area that crossed the VGN. In an exchange of trackage rights, VGN received access to downtown Norfolk over two miles of NS and built a freight house. Between 1910 and 1912 the N&W, VGN and NS con-structed a new passenger station in downtown Norfolk. VGN passenger trains moved to NS rails at Tidewater Tower for the trip to and from the new station. The crossing was an inter-locking manned by NS employees and was known as "Tidewater" in VGN timetables. On July 3, 1955 childhood bud-dies Wally Johnson and August Thieme were at Tidewater to record Train #4 pulled by PA Class Pacific 215.

LEFT and RIGHT • Eastbound VGN passenger trains pulled into Terminal Station head first, and then backed out after unloading and ran to Sewells Point for servicing and a layover until the next day. Westbound trains would back into the station from Tidewater. In the first photo Train #4 with PA Class Pacific 215 has backed out from the station and is on the connecting track from the NS to the VGN. In the next photo the photogra-pher is standing on the NS track looking east as #4 begins backing past Tidewater on its way to Sewells Point.

(Two photos, A. Thieme)

LEFT • The photographer was facing north up VGN's double track main as #4 backed past Tidewater and crossed over to the east main on July 3, 1955.

(D. Wallace Johnson)

ABOVE • On August 21, 1955 Train #3 was leaving Terminal Station for its seven and one half hour run to Roanoke with a baggage/RPO car and an air-conditioned N&W coach behind PA Class Pacific 213. We will cover both the trains and the engines later, for now this beautiful scene shows the stub end nature of the station and its relatively small size. The train has five months left. (*A. Thieme*)

ABOVE • As the last road built in the Norfolk area, the Virginian had to contend with both the city and the lines of other railroads. It laid out a path that took it around the city, between Norfolk and Virginia Beach, and then west far south of the city. In so doing it crossed the Eastern Branch of the Elizabeth River just south of Tidewater on a bridge/trestle combination with a swing span. On July 3, 1955 the train we saw earlier at Tidewater was traveling north (east by timetable) across the Eastern Branch. (*A. Thieme*)

The Virginian was organized in two divisions: the Norfolk Division from Sewells Point to Roanoke and the New River Division from Roanoke to Deepwater. The Norfolk Division was further divided into the First Subdivision from Sewells Point to the town of Victoria, 119.7 miles from Terminal Station, and the Second Subdivision from Victoria 123.4 miles west to Roanoke. In common usage east of Roanoke was the "East End" and west to Deepwater was the "West End". Speed limits were generally 55 MPH for passenger trains, 45 MPH for time freights and locals and 35 MPH for all other trains. After 1946 movement between Sewells Point and South Branch Yard was gov-erned by Centralized Traffic Control with searchlight signals. From South Branch west the East End was strictly a rule book, timetable and train order operation until the end.

RIGHT • Time Table No. 21 from May 2, 1948 carried two through passenger trains, nos. 3 and 4, two daily time freights, 71/72, and two locals on alternates days, 31/32. Here is page 1 showing the stations of the First Subdivision.
(N&WHS Archives)

BELOW • On its way west the VGN had numerous industrial/business sidings in the Norfolk area. It operated a local freight from Sewells Point to a small yard called "South Branch" just across the Southern Branch of the Elizabeth River. The yard limits for the Norfolk area stretched from Sewells Point to milepost 9.5 just west of South Branch Yard. In this undated photo from the mid-1950s the South Branch local is heading north in Norfolk behind an MB as the rear brakeman surveys the scene. *(Harry Bundy)*

First Sub-Division—Sewells Point to Victoria

TIME TABLE No. 21 — Effective 12:01 A. M., May 2, 1948

Hours T. O. Offices are Open	Coal, Water, Turning Facilities	Station Number	Miles from Norfolk	STATIONS	WESTWARD First Class 3 Daily Passenger	WESTWARD 2nd Class 71 Daily Time Freight	WESTWARD Third Class 31 Tue.-Thur.-Sat. Local Freight	EASTWARD First Class 4 Daily Passenger	EASTWARD 2nd Class 72 Daily Time Freight	EASTWARD Third Class 32 Mon.Wed.Fri. Local Freight
					AM—L.	PM—L.	AM—L.	PM—A.	AM—A.	PM—A.
Continuous	CWT	A8	10	SEWELLS POINT	7 26	9 00	7 00	4 30	5 45	3 20
		A7.2	9.5	WEST JUNCTION — N. & P. BELT LINE R. R. 1.3	7 26			4 29		
	Y	A5.9	8.2	Q. M. JUNCTION — STREET CAR CROSSING, FAIRMONT PARK 4.5	7 28			4 27		
Continuous		A1.4	3.7	COLEMAN PLACE — N. S. RY. CROSSING INTERLOCKED 1.4	7 39			4 16		
Continuous		2	2.3	TIDEWATER — N. S. RY. CROSSING INTERLOCKED 2.3	7 40			4 15	5 15	2 44
		0	...	NORFOLK TERM. STATION — N. & W. RY.	8 00			4 00		
		2	2.3	TIDEWATER — N. S. RY. CROSSING INTERLOCKED EASTERN BRANCH DRAWBRIDGE INTRLKD. 2.2	8 10	9 16	7 20	3 50		
Continuous		4.5	4.5	CAROLINA — N. S. RY. CROSSING INTERLOCKED 0.6	f 8 16	9 20	7 28	f 3 44	4 53	2 35
Continuous		5	5.1	SOUTH NORFOLK — N. & W. RY. CROSSING INTERLOCKED 1.4	8 17			3 43		
		6.5	6.5	BELT JUNCTION — N. & P. BELT LINE R. R. CROSSING INTERLOCKED, SOUTH BRANCH DRAWBRIDGE INTERLOCKED 0.9	8 19			3 40		
	WY	7	7.4	SOUTH BRANCH 6.2	8 22	9 50	7 35	3 38	4 38	2 25
		13.5	13.6	SUNRAY 1.8	f 8 31			f 3 28		
		15	15.4	ALGREN — S. A. L. R. R. CROSS'G—AUTOMATICALLY INTERLKD. 2.4	f 8 34	10 03	7 53	f 3 26	4 26	2 05
		21		MAGNOLIA 2.4	f 8 44			f 3 16		
Continuous		24	23.5	SUFFOLK 4.2	s 8 49	10 20	8 20	s 3 11	4 15	1 45
		28	27.7	KENYON 6.1	f 8 56	10 27	8 30	f 3 05	3 43	12 48
		34	33.8	BOAZ 3.4	f 9 04	10 36	8 46	f 2 56	3 33	12 35
		37	37.2	COLOSSE 1.9	f 9 10			f 2 50		
8.00 A. M. to 5.00 P. M. ★		39	39.0	WALTERS 2.4	s 9 14			s 2 46		
		41	41.4	BURDETTE 5.0	s 9 20 31	10 46	9 20 3	s 2 42	3 21	12 15
9.00 A. M. to 6.00 P. M.		47	46.4	SEDLEY 1.4	s 9 28	10 53	9 35	s 2 33	3 13	12 01PM
8.00 P. M. to 5.00 A. M. ★	OW	48	47.8	MORGAN 7.2	f 9 30	11 03	9 45	f 2 31	3 11	11 50AM
5.00 A. M. to 5.00 P. M. ★		54	54.3	SEBRELL 7.3	s 9 41	11 13	10 10	s 2 15	3 01	11 28
★ 5.00 P. M.		62	61.5	JOYNER 5.3	s 9 54	11 23	10 29	s 2 02	2 50	11 00
		67	66.8	GRAY — A. C. L. R. R. CROSSING INTERLOCKED 7.0	s 10 04	11 32	10 45	s 1 52	2 41	10 45
Continuous — 8.00 A. M. to 5.00 P. M. ★		74	73.7	JARRATT 6.3	s 10 15 32	11 50PM	11 15	s 1 41	2 30	10 15 3
8.00 A. M. to 5.00 P. M. ★		81	80.7	PURDY 6.3	s 10 30	12 03AM	11 30	s 1 30	1 29	9 50
★ 5.00 P. M.		87	87.0	ADBIT 2.0	s 10 42	12 13	11 45AM	s 1 21	1 19	9 34
		89	89.0	SMOKY ORDINARY 3.0	f 10 46			f 1 17		
		92	92.0	DOLPHIN 5.9	s 10 51	12 19	12 05PM	s 1 12	1 10	9 13
Continuous	W	98	97.9	ALBERTA 4.9	s 11 01	12 45 72	1 00 4	s 1 00 31	1 00 71AM	8 50
8.00 A. M. to 5.00 P. M. ★		103	102.8	DANIELTOWN 3.7	f 11 09			f 12 53		
5.45 A. M. to 6.00 P. M. ★		107	106.5	DUNDAS 6.9	s 11 17	12 57	1 30	s 12 45	11 51PM	8 05
		113	113.4	KENBRIDGE 6.3	s 11 30	1 09	2 00	s 12 33	11 41	7 40
Continuous	CWT	120	119.7	VICTORIA	s 11 45	1 25	2 20	12 20	11 30	7 00
					AM—A.	AM—A.	PM—A.	PM—L.	PM—L.	AM—L.

★Daily except Sunday.

ABOVE • MB 430 was in charge of the South Branch Local in December 1954, making a pickup/setout in Norfolk. The 430 had a road pilot, without the black and white safety stripes seen earlier on some MBs assigned to Sewells Point.

(H. Reid, collection of A. Thieme)

BELOW • On November 7, 1954 Train #3 was leaving Norfolk behind PA 210, which showed signs of being wiped down with fish oil between runs. The Pacific was built by Alco's Richmond Works in 1920. It was rare at this late date to see three cars on Trains 3 and 4, Virginian's last passenger schedules. *(Russell F. Munroe, Jr.)*

ABOVE • Just south of the N&W's merchandise yard at Portlock in the city of Chesapeake, the Virginian crossed the N&W's double-tracked mainline at South Norfolk interlocking. In November 1958 four DE-S Class H16-44s were eastbound with a coal train from Victoria about to cross the N&W. *(Bob Clarkson)*

VGN ALGREN

ABOVE • After leaving South Branch Yard and the Norfolk metropolitan area, the VGN headed west on a long tangent along the north edge of the Great Dismal Swamp. The Seaboard Air Line track from Portsmouth followed a generally southwest course and the two lines crossed at grade at Algren, milepost 15.4. Algren was also the point at which the Tidewater Railway began westward construction of its line to Victoria in 1905. On January 2, 1955 BA Class 2-8-4 506 was westbound approaching the SAL crossing at Algren with a train of empties that appear to be C&O or Clinchfield offset side hoppers.

(H. Reid, collection of A. Thieme)

After crossing the SAL at Algren, VGN ran parallel to the other road to and through Suffolk, milepost 23.5. Suffolk was a small city with an agricultural base through which five railroads passed. The ACL and the Atlantic & Danville passed over the Virginian on their way to their Elizabeth River terminals on the Portsmouth side of the river, and the N&W passed through Suffolk to the south of SAL and VGN. The Virginian had a short section of track that ran into downtown Suffolk to reach industries and business was brisk enough to base a switcher there until the merger. Thereafter and for some years an N&W unit was stationed in Suffolk.

ABOVE • The light industrial track in Suffolk required light power. For many years, SA Class 0-8-0s #2 or 4 held down the Suffolk assignment. On March 7, 1954 the 2 was resting in Suffolk with its boiler glistening from a fish oil rubdown. She was displaced in the coming summer by Alco/GE 44-tonner 6 and was scrapped in 1955.

(A. Thieme)

LEFT • In an image recorded on early half-frame 35mm Kodachrome, H. Reid captured SA 4 and caboose 85 at Suffolk in April 1953. *(H. Reid)*

ABOVE • As VGN dieselized in 1954, it was clear that the new Fairbanks-Morse H16-44s purchased for the East End were too heavy for the Suffolk assignment. To handle the task VGN purchased an Alco/GE 44-ton switcher from R.C. Stanhope Company and numbered it 6. It held down the Suffolk assignment until 1960, when it was sold to Eastern Gas & Fuel Associates. In this undated photo we see it at work in Suffolk. *(Courtesy of Bob's Photo)*

BELOW • A very rare photo shows the 6 after it was sold to EG&F, sitting at Norfolk on August 6, 1960.

(Bob Clarkson)

ABOVE • The Virginian was built to haul coal to Tidewater in the most efficient manner possible. As the line was extended west it passed through the sparsely populated, largely agricultural area of southern Virginia known locally as "Southside". It was then, and remains a pastoral landscape, bereft of industry, but suitable for a low grade railroad. The builders of the Tidewater/Virginian no doubt had some interest in manifest traffic, but it could not have been very high for they bypassed the population centers where industries tend-ed to spring up. So the VGN had a modest amount of mixed freight traffic, much of it interlined with other carriers. At the small town of Jarratt, 74 miles west of Norfolk and due south of Richmond, the VGN crossed the double-tracked north-south speedway of the Atlantic Coast Line. VGN had a small yard at Jarrett and inter-changed a fair amount of traffic with the ACL. In the mid-1950s Train #4 behind PA 215 was approaching Jarratt at track speed.

(Steve Bogen)

No state, save perhaps Massachusetts, has its history more intertwined with "Olde England" than Virginia. Parse a map of the state and one will find the names of English historical figures everywhere, including the town of Victoria, created as part of the construction of the Tidewater Railway and named by none other than H. H. Rogers for Queen Victoria. The Tidewater began heading west from Algren in 1905 and 104 miles later, in 1907, it built the town of Victoria to serve as its division point. The new town was almost halfway between Norfolk and Roanoke. In the days of 100-mile crew districts, it was a day's work from either terminal. And in the Virginian operating pattern Victoria was the home terminal for all East End road crews; they were qualified on both the First and Second Subs and were called out in either direction. Victoria had several long yard tracks, an engine facility with a small roundhouse, and an imposing two-story station that also housed the offices of the Norfolk Division and the East End dispatchers. While some manifest switching took place, the principal functions of Victoria were to change crews and to stage coal drags for Sewells Point. Today one has trouble finding any physical indication that a major Virginian facility was once an important part of the local economy, but the townspeople still find ways to recognize the road's presence.

ABOVE • In the earliest image in this volume, taken in 1950, four steel cabs rest in front of the station/office building in Victoria. When H. Reid began to take color slides, he started with a half-frame 35mm format, from which this image is taken. *(H. Reid)*

BELOW • On May 23, 1953 Train #4 behind PA 214 was kicking up yard dust at the west end of the Victoria yard, slowing for its 12:10 PM stop. The train left Roanoke at 8:00 AM and was scheduled into Norfolk at 4:30 PM. By 1955 the train will be down from three to two cars as the road tries to discontinue the service. *(A. Thieme)*

ABOVE • A little over a year later, on July 13, 1954, Thieme, as he is known, was standing in the kudzu as #4 approached Victoria behind PA 210. The last car appears to be an N&W coach, which we will discuss shortly. For those not familiar with kudzu, a virulent weed found throughout the South, let us just say that if Thieme hung around this spot very long, the kudzu would start growing up his leg! In any event, this scene is typical of the land through which VGN passed in Southside Virginia; flat, red clay, and kudzu. A land of corn, tobacco and, some say, the finest 'homebrewed' liquor in the country. *(A. Thieme)*

ABOVE • MCA 484 was under steam at Victoria on June 1, 1953. The engine was built in 1912 as MC Class 463 and rebuilt and renumbered in May 1941. After consultation with Baldwin, between 1937 and 1941 Princeton Shops added disc drivers and light-weight rods supplied by Baldwin to five Class MC engines to produce MCA Class 480-484. The boiler pressure was raised to 200 pounds, giving them a tractive effort of 64,500 pounds, 3300 pounds more than the MC Class. The improvements enabled the five engines to handle time freights on the East End at faster speeds. *(Collection of Morning Sun Books)*

LEFT • At the east end of Victoria, with the two-story station peeking above the train in the distance, MB 2-8-2 430 switched a long cut of the road's famous "battleship" coal gondolas. The gondolas and the MB were largely the product of George Halstead, the road's Chief Draftsman. After VGN experiment-ed in the teens with several 120-ton coal gondolas, in the early 1920s Pressed Steel Car Company began delivering G-class 116-ton coal gondolas riding on custom-designed six-wheel Buckeye trucks. They were used in mine-to-pier service until the merger with the N&W, although their numbers diminished in the later years. The 430 carries a road pilot and its original square cab. It lacks the spark arrestor and other signs of tender care by shop forces we saw on the MBs used in yard service at Sewells Point. Observers of the Virginian in steam days noted that the shop forces in Norfolk seemed to give special touches to their power; fish oil rubdowns, and alu-minum paint here and there. *(A. Thieme)*

RIGHT • AG Class 2-6-6-6 903 was resting at Victoria on May 23, 1953 when Thieme framed its imposing front end. All eight AGs were scrapped by the N&W in January 1960, one month after the merger.

(A. Thieme)

"Once a day, Nutbush, Va., was a roaring fast place."
H. Reid, *The Virginian Railway*, 1961

ABOVE and BELOW • Five and a half miles west of Victoria was a rural passing siding that went by the name of Nutbush, for reasons lost to time. What prompted Reid's eloquence? Well, Trains 3 and 4 were scheduled to pass there around mid-day. On April 3, 1953 Train #3 approached the east end of the siding at Nutbush behind PA 4-6-2 212, then passed Train #4 waiting impatiently behind PA 214, the shined number board of which shows the careful attention these racehorses received. *(Two photos, A. Thieme)*

ABOVE and BELOW • Six miles west of Nutbush, at milepost 131.5, was the village of Meherrin, boyhood home of one of the great guitar pickers of all time, Roy Clark. At Meherrin the Richmond to Danville line of the Southern passed over the Virginian. On May 16, 1954 Train #4 was passing through Meherrin behind the 212 with the customary Pullman Green baggage/RPO leading two coaches. Ten months later, on March 12, 1955, the 210 on Train #3 was rip- ping through Meherrin at track speed under a clear stack with the Southern crossing in the background. Careful observers will notice that 210 carried a different numberboard from that seen on 212 and 215 in earlier images. It also appears that part of the running board and the Prime Cylinder Protection Valves on top of the cylinders had received fresh aluminum paint. *(Two photos, A. Thieme)*

LEFT, TOP TO BOTTOM • During the Christmas holidays in 1953 August Thieme traveled to Meherrin, Virginia, a flag stop about twelve miles west of Victoria to capture Trains #3 and #4 before they disappeared. At that time the Virginian was trying to get the Commonwealth of Virginia to permit discontinuance of the trains. In this first sequence we see the agent and perhaps a pal waiting for the arrival of #4, which was scheduled into Meherrin 23 minutes before #3. Not much mail or express was ready to move eastbound this day. PA 214 sent coal smoke skyward as it eased away from the station, and then rounded the curve with the usual three car consist on December 26, 1953. *(Three photos, A. Thieme)*

ABOVE • Before the arrival of #3, Thieme recorded this beautiful image of the station with mail and express waiting to go west. This is one of the best color images of the last Virginian paint scheme for structures and maintenance of way equipment, medium gray with brown trim. Earlier the paint would have been deep orange with white trim. *(A. Thieme)*

PASSENGER
SCHEDULES
and
INFORMATION

Virginian
Railway

VGN

J. SCHMUCK, JR.
General Passenger Agent

C. T. FISHER, JR.
Passenger Representative

Norfolk 10, Va.

LEFT and ABOVE • At 11:54 AM, as advertised, PA 212 brought #3 to a brief stop at Meherrin, and then accelerated away smartly. Thieme does not recall how many enginemen were in the cab, but since the head-end brakeman would have been riding the train, it appears that the engineer has left his right hand spot to give the photographer a wave! *(Three photos A. Thieme)*

ABOVE • Two miles west of Meherrin was Virso, taking its name from <u>Vir</u>ginian and <u>So</u>uthern, which shared a connection there. On September 7, 1953 PA 214 was leading Train #4 east on jointed rail with a ballast line that shows careful attention by the section crew. *(A. Thieme)*

VGN CULLEN

ABOVE • West of Virso, at milepost 150.7, was this small structure, which served as a flagstop station and freight "house". The building wears a well-worn coat of Virginian gray and brown paint.

(Aubrey Wiley, collection of Bill McClure)

Let us pause for a moment on our journey west and look at the last new steam power built for the railroad. At the beginning of World War II traffic on Virginian's East End was being handled as follows: massive 2-10-10-2s originally built for pusher service on the West End worked coal drags between Roanoke and Victoria; 700-series USRA-designed compound 2-8-8-2s worked coal between Victoria and Sewells Point; 2-8-2s handled the time freights and locals; PA Class Pacifics worked passenger trains and time freights; and TA Class 4-6-0s handled passenger trains. The work got done, but speed was not part of the equation. The AE Class 2-10-10-2s could take from 12 to 15 hours to travel the 125 miles between Roanoke and Victoria! As Tidewater-bound traffic boomed during the War, East End time freights were double-headed by two MBs or an MB and a PA. In short, the Virginian was a classic drag-era railroad; big tonnage at slow but consistent speeds. It did differ from most drag-era roads in one important respect; it made money by the hopper load.

The Virginian did not compete for fast merchandise, nor did it compete for passenger business. It was built to haul coal and to do so it had always believed in extremely powerful locomotives as measured by tractive effort. As productive as they were, not one of its engines would have been considered "modern" in any way when World War II began. It had never felt the need to embrace the "Superpower" concepts developed by Lima in the mid-1920s. In 1944 that began to change. Beginning in 1942 several senior managers of C&O left the railroad as a result of policies implemented by its new Chairman, Robert R. Young. First to leave was George D. Brooke, former C&O President, who became Chairman of the Virginian Board of Directors. In May 1944 Frank D. Beale, a former C&O Vice President and Assistant to the President, left his position at the Nickel Plate and became Virginian's

President. It should not have surprised anyone when in June 1944 VGN's Board authorized the purchase of 8 huge 2-6-6-6s from Lima to be built to the plans of the C&O's H-8 class, with a few changes. Delivery of the first order of C&O's H-8s had begun in 1941 when Brooke and Beale were senior C&O executives, so they knew the design well and had seen its stunning performance on heavy coal trains. In C&O tests the new design delivered 7600 horsepower at the drawbar, with a continuous rating of 6000 horsepower at 35 MPH. In terms of pure horsepower, it has been written that they were the most powerful steam locomotives ever produced.

The new Virginian locomotives were delivered in 1945 and immediately reduced running times. An AG was said to take empty trains of 4500 tons from Victoria to Roanoke in 4 hours 50 minutes and to haul 14,500 ton coal trains from Victoria to Sewells Point in just less than four hours. While steam locomotive experts long have argued that the immense horsepower capability of C&O's H-8s was wasted in slow-speed coal train service, an argument that applies to the VGN as well, there is no denying that the H-8s and AGs did exactly what the roads expected and did it spectacularly. The AGs spent their short service lives in coal train service between Roanoke and Sewells Point until diesels arrived in 1954.

In compiling the photography for this volume, one of the mysteries has been the lack of color action shots of the AGs and the later BA Class Berkshires. Photographers of that era have told your authors that East End trains tended to run at night, that Virginian ran few trains, and that the nearby N&W main was so much busier that steam fans tended to stay where the action was assured. Whatever the reasons, we are pleased to be able to add these outstanding images to the published record of the railroad.

ABOVE • In January 1955 AG 905 was resting at Sewells Point. The first VGN diesels arrived in 1954 and subsequent orders came in 1956-57. Within the year 905 will be stored and, following the N&W merger, will be sold for scrap in January 1960. *(H. Reid)*

ABOVE • Not many things are as painful for a railfan as a steam locomotive awaiting the scrap yard. We present this image to show the beautifully balanced bulk of one of Lima's finest products. The AG was of a design so utterly compact, yet still so massive that air tanks had to be located atop the firebox and the twin Westinghouse air pumps, in a departure from Lima styling, were mounted on the smokebox door. The principal spotting differences between a C&O H-8 and a VGN AG: the sand domes on the AG were somewhat smaller and the tender water cistern was taller on the AG, with a pronounced roll to the top edge. The C&O tender carried 25 tons of coal and 25,000 gallons of water; the AG tenders carried 26,500 gallons of water with the same coal capacity. 902 rested at Sewells Point on January 22, 1956, some two years after being displaced by diesels on the East End. *(D. Wallace Johnson)*

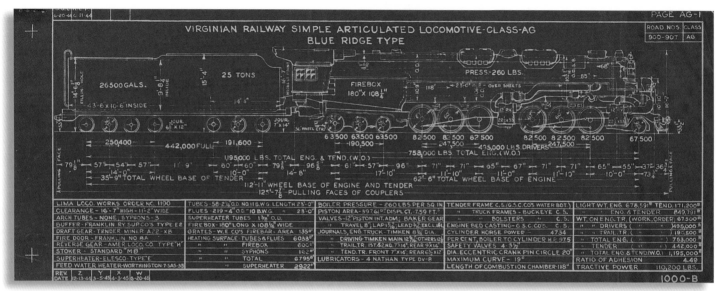

ABOVE • On the Virginian the AG was called the "Blue Ridge" in honor of the mountains of western Virginia, but the name never really took root. Here is the diagram sheet for the AG class, as of June 20, 1945. *(Collection of Bill McClure)*

ABOVE • After the demise of steam, numerous VGN locomotives could be found at the main shops in Princeton, West Virginia. Some had been shopped just prior to diesels arriving and were stored in pristine condition. In June 1959 AG 906 was sitting out of service at the end of the Princeton transfer table, but looking as if she were ready for an eastbound. It has been speculated that the Virginian intended to donate the 906, but then the merger came and N&W moved rapidly to scrap the remaining VGN steam. All 8 AGs were sold for scrap in January 1960. From this view the principal spotting differences between the AG and the C&O H-8 are clear: larger AG tender, but smaller sand domes. *(Roger F. Whitt)*

In 1943 the C&O took delivery from Alco of the first 40 of what would become 90 Class K-4 Berkshires, named "Kanawhas" on the C&O. The engines were the culmination of developments in steam power that began with the first "Superpower" 2-8-4 in 1925. During the 1920s and '30s the C&O, Erie, Nickel Plate and Pere Marquette were under the control of the Van Sweringen brothers, whose Advisory Mechanical Committee coordinated development of mechanical standards for each road. The AMC had developed high-capacity 2-8-4s for the Erie, NKP and PM, and in 1930 had scaled up the Erie's 1927 2-8-4 to produce the famous T-1 2-10-4 for C&O coal traffic. The T-1s were so successful that the design was scaled down in 1934 to produce the equally famous S class 2-8-4 for the Nickel Plate; high speed manifest haulers for the NKP Chicago racetrack.

Although the AMC was gone by the 1940s as Robert Young gained control of the C&O, the proven designs of the former AMC roads were used to produce the K-4 in 1944. Just as

Messrs. Brooke and Beale had seen first hand the capabilities of the huge H-8s, so too they had followed the development of C&O's finest flatland power. To improve running times on the VGN East End time freights they again turned to Lima for five 2-8-4s that were virtually identical in principal specifications, excluding the trailing truck booster, to the K-4s produced by Lima. The BAs rode 69" drivers, carried a boiler pressure of 245 psi and developed 69,350 pounds of tractive effort. Visually they differed from their C&O brethren in having a combined steam/sand dome and carrying larger tenders with a rolled top edge on the water cistern. The BAs took over time freights 71-74 from the MBs and MCAs and immediately reduced running times. H. Reid recounts a tale of BA 505 detouring over the N&W, presumably over the racetrack between Norfolk and Petersburg, with 3500 tons at 87 MPH! Alas, they were still young when all were scrapped by the N&W in 1960.

ABOVE • BA 506 at rest at Sewells Point in January 1955 exudes "speed". In several photos taken at Sewells Point we see a steam-cleaned front-ends ahead of the light gray road grime produced by heavy use of sand or traction. *(H. Reid)*

LEFT • The most photographed Virginian steam surely must have been the few engines displayed by the road during the 1957 National Railway Historical Society Convention in Roanoke. PA 212, AG 907 and BA 507 were sparkling, as we shall see later. A year after that convention, George Dimond made this beautiful low-light study of the face of 507 as it sat forlornly near the Roanoke roundhouse, no longer a display piece.

(George Dimond)

By the 1950s passenger service was down to nos. 3 and 4, with two train sets working Norfolk-Roanoke and two working Roanoke-Deepwater, and Virginian was working the regulatory processes to discontinue all passenger services. The run into Charleston was discontinued in January 1952, and service was then cut back from Deepwater to Page in June of that year. West Virginia then allowed service west of Princeton to be discontinued in 1953.

In 1954 the Virginia regulators permitted service west of Roanoke to be discontinued, but required the VGN to continue operation of 3 and 4 on the East End for another year, but with improved service, which meant closed windows and air conditioning! So in this volume the reader will see a leased N&W air conditioned coach on the rear of Trains 3 and 4 during 1955. After a year of "improved" service, the road was permitted to discontinue the last chapter of Virginian passenger service, which it did with style on January 29, 1956. PAs 212 and 213 did the honors, with the meet in Victoria instead of the regular Nutbush passing, and in so doing became the last Virginian steam operated on a regular basis.

"The State Corporation of Virginia authorized the discontinuance of passenger-train service between Norfolk and Roanoke effective January 29, 1956. This completes the elimination of the unproductive and costly passenger-train operation by the company."

President Frank D. Beale, 1956 Annual Report

On that unsentimental note, the Virginian exited the passenger train business.

Virginian Railway Company

TIME TABLE No. 13

Superseding Time Table No. 12, dated November 17, 1929

Taking Effect Sunday,
May 11, 1930,
at 12:01 o'clock A. M.

For the Government and Information of Employee Only; Not for the Public

C. H. HIX, President   GEO. MASTEN, General Superintendent   J. W. WHITE, Superintendent   B. L. PEDNEAU, Superintendent

4 Third and Fourth East Sub-Divisions—NEW RIVER DIVISION

63 Ex. Sun. Local Freight (Third Class)	15 Daily. Passenger (First Class)	3 Daily. Passenger (First Class)	5 Daily. Passenger (First Class)	Miles from Norfolk	Station Numbers	Car Capacity of other Tracks	Car Capacity of Sidings	STATIONS	Telegraph Calls	Telegraph Stations	Coal, Water, Scales, Turn Table, Wye	12 Daily. Passenger	4 Daily. Passenger	6 Daily. Passenger	64 Ex. Sun. Local Freight
A.M.-lv. 7.00	A.M.-lv. 9.30			243.1	243			★....ROANOKE.... 3.7	JK RO	DN	C.W. S.T.Y		P.M.-ar. 7.15		P.M.-ar. 5.50
	9.39			246.8	247	20		★....BELT LINE.... NORFOLK & WESTERN RY. 3.8					7.06		
s 7.20	s 9.47			250.6	251	45	124	★....SALEM.... 6.0	SA	DN			s 6.58		s 3.00
f 7.35	f 9.58			256.6	257	7	113	★....WABUN.... 4.2					f 6.47		f 2.37
f 7.45	f 10.06			260.8	261	10	112	★....KUMIS.... 5.5			W		f 6.38		f 2.25
f 8.00	s 10.17			266.3	266	10	124	★....IRONTO.... 3.3					s 6.27		f 2.11
s 8.10	f 10.24			269.6	270	78	110	★....FAGG.... 2.6			W Y		f 6.20		f 2.01
s 8.18	f 10.30			272.4	272	16		★....ELLETT.... 3.9	DA	DN			s 6.15		f 1.55
f 8.25	f 10.39			276.3	276	4	72	★....YELLOW SULPHUR.... 2.0					f 6.06		f 1.40
s 8.35	s 10.44			278.3	278			★....MERRIMAC.... NORFOLK & WESTERN RY. 0.8	MC	D			s 6.01		f 1.35
f 8.40	10.46			279.1	279	9	128	★....SHELBY.... 5.1					6.00		f 1.33
f 8.51	f 10.57			284.2	284	14	124	★....PRICE.... 3.5					s 5.50		1.20
f 9.10	s 11.05			287.7	288	100	119	★....WHITETHORNE.... 5.0	WN	DN	C.W. Y		s 5.42		f 1.10
s 9.25	f 11.15			292.7	293	58	124	★....McCOY.... 5.5					f 5.32		f 12.55
s 9.45	s 11.25			298.2	298	23	113	★....EGGLESTON.... 5.2	SY	D	W		s 5.21		f 12.35
f 10.00	s 11.35			303.4	303	13	124	★....PEMBROKE.... 3.9	RM	D			s 5.10		f 12.20 PM
f 10.10	f 11.43			307.3	307	100		★....KLOTZ.... NORFOLK & WESTERN RY. 1.9			S		f 5.02		f
f 10.15	s 11.49 (64)			309.2	309	7	143	★....NORCROSS.... 4.9	CS	W			s 4.58		f 11.49 (3)
f 10.30	f 11.59 AM			314.1	314	3	132	★....NORTH PEARISBURG.... 3.3					f 4.48		f 11.37
f 10.45	s 12.07 PM			317.4	317	60		★....NARROWS.... 3.4					4.41		f 11.25
s 11.10 (64)	s 12.15			320.8	321	16	112	★....RICH CREEK.... 7.0	RC	DN			s 4.33		s 11.10 (63)
f 11.45 AM	12.30			327.8	328	25	124	★....KELLYSVILLE.... 3.6			W		s 4.17		f 10.20
12.01 PM	12.39			331.4	331	21		★....STENGLE.... 3.8					4.08		10.10
12.20	f 12.48			335.2	335		91	★....INGLESIDE.... 5.0					4.00		10.00
1.20	P.M.-lv. 6.00	(1.00 (63) / 1.10)	A.M.-lv. 5.50	340.2	340			★....PRINCETON.... 4.8	Q	DN	C W STY	A.M.-ar. 8.35	(3.50 / 3.40)	P.M.-ar. 8.55	P.M.-ar. 9.45
1.43	f 6.10	s 1.20	s 6.00	345.0	345	20	115	★....KEGLEY.... 3.6	GY	D		s 8.23	s 3.29	s 8.44	9.20
2.00	f 6.17	f 1.27	f 6.07	348.6	349	18	114	★....KING.... 3.2			W	f 8.14	f 3.21	f 8.36	9.05
f 2.15	f 6.23	f 1.33	f 6.13	351.5	352	6	135	★....ROCK.... 4.0				f 8.08	f 3.14	f 8.29	f 8.56
2.30 (4)	6.32	1.42 (4)	6.22	355.5	355			★....M. X. TOWER.... 0.7	MX	DN		7.59	3.05 (3-63)	8.20	8.45
s.	s 6.34	1.45	s 6.24	356.2	356	12		★....MATOAKA.... 0.6	K	D		7.57	s 3.02	8.17	s.
f.	6.36	1.47	6.26	356.8	357	16		★....N. & W. TRANSFER.... 4.0				7.55	3.00	8.15	f.
3.15	6.44	1.57	6.34	360.8	360	160		★....CLARK'S GAP TOWER.... 1.2	CG	DN	W	7.46	2.47	8.06	8.15
	6.48	2.01	6.38	362.0	362		75	★....MILE POST 362.... 1.6				7.41	2.41	8.01	
	6.51	2.04	6.41	363.6	364			★....MICAJAH.... 4.2				7.37	2.37	f 7.57	
f 4.00	7.02	2.16	6.52	367.8	368	62		★....HERNDON.... 3.3	H	DN	W	7.25	2.25	f 7.45	7.45
	7.12	2.26	s 7.02	371.1	371			★....BUD.... 0.9				7.14	s 2.14	f 7.34	
	7.19	2.29	7.10	372.0	373	80		★....ALPOCA.... 2.7				7.10	2.10	7.30	
4.30 P.M.-ar.	7.25 P.M.-ar.	2.38 (64) / 7.14 P.M.-ar.	7.14 A.M.-ar.	374.7	375			★....ELMORE....	MO	DN	CWY	7.00 A.M.-lv.	2.01 P.M.-lv.	7.21 P.M.-lv.	7.10 (5-12) A.M.-lv.
9:30	1:25	5:08	1:24					Running Time				1:35	5:14	1:34	8:20

ABOVE, LEFT and TOP RIGHT • The Virginian was built to haul coal, not passengers. Nevertheless, from its beginnings it operated a modest number of passenger trains, most of which were "accommodation" runs that serviced the local needs of its sparsely populated country via many flagstops. It did operate what it called "through trains" with sleeping accommodations between Norfolk and Deepwater, situated on the south bank of the Kanawha River, and then on to Charleston, West Virginia. At first the Charleston leg was handled via a connection with the C&O at Deepwater. Later Virginian's trains ran into Charleston via the New York Central, with whom VGN connected on the north bank of the Kanawha. In 1930 Employee Timetable No. 13 revealed four daily through passenger trains on the New River Division; Trains 3 and 4, operating daily between Roanoke and Deepwater, and Trains 5 and 6 running daily between Princeton and Deepwater. By the end of the 1930s nearly all of the locals and mixed trains that served the coal branches were gone.

(N&WHS Archives)

Time Table No. 13 — TAKING EFFECT SUNDAY, MAY 11TH, 1930

1 (Daily)	65 Exc. Sun. Local Freight	15 Daily Pass.	3 Daily Pass.	11 Daily Pass.	5 Daily Pass.	Miles from Norfolk	Sta. No.	Other Tracks	Sidings	STATIONS	Tel. Calls	Tel. Sta.	Coal/Water/Scales/Turn Table/Wye	12 Daily Pass.	4 Daily Pass.	6 Daily Pass.	16 Daily Pass.	66 Exc. Sun. Local Freight	62 Daily
	A.M.-lv. 8.15	P.M.-lv. 7.25 (16 6)	s P.M.-lv. 2.38	A.M.-lv. 7.25 (12)	A.M.-lv. 7.14 (12)	374.7	375			★ ELMORE (DOUBLE TRACK)	MO	DN	C.W. Y	s A.M.-ar. 7.00 (5 11)	s P.M.-ar. 2.01	P.M.-ar. 7.21	P.M.-ar. 7.10 (15)	P.M.-ar. 1.40	
	8.25	7.30	2.43	7.29	7.18	376.5				★ GULF JUNCTION	J	DN		6.55 A.M.-lv.	1.56	7.16	7.05 P.M.-lv.	1.30	
	s 8.35	7.31 P.M.-ar.	2.55	7.30 A.M.-ar.	7.21	376.7	377	59		★ MULLENS			Y		1.55	7.15		1.25	
	f		s 3.00		f 7.26	378.1	378	30		NURIVA					s 1.37	f 7.02			
	f		f 3.01		f 7.27	378.5	379	38		CALORIC					s 1.35	f 7.00			
	f		3.04		f 7.31	379.3	380	44		OTSEGO					s 1.32	f 6.58			
	9.00		3.07		7.34	380.4	381			VIRWEST					1.29	6.55		12.55	
	s 9.25		s 3.17		s 7.38	381.7	382	74	158	★ MABEN	B	D	W		s 1.26	6.51		s 12.45 PM	
	f 9.40		s 3.27		s 7.46	385.6	386	6	73	★ HOTCHKISS					s 1.16	f 6.41		s 11.45 AM	
	f 10.00		s 3.35		s 7.52	387.9	388	139	81	★ SLAB FORK	BF	DN			s 1.09	s 6.34		s 11.30	
	f 10.10		3.41		f 7.57	390.1	390	1	71	★ JENNY GAP					1.03	6.29		f 11.15	
	10.25		3.44		8.00	391.7	391		27	LESTER SIDING					12.58	6.24		11.10	
	s 10.35		s 3.48		s 8.03	392.2	392	16		★ LESTER	RB	D			s 12.56	6.22		s 11.05	
	s 10.50 (66)		s 3.55		s 8.10	394.6	395	39	71	★ SURVEYOR	RJ	D	W		s 12.49	6.16		s 10.50 (65)	
	f 11.05		4.00		8.13	396.3	396		47	GLEN WHITE JUNCTION			Y		12.44	6.12		f 10.40	
	f		4.03		f 8.15	396.9	397	60		METALTON					f 12.43	6.10		f	
	s 11.30		s 4.08		8.19	398.6	399	10		★ ECCLES	KA	D			s 12.38	6.06		s 10.30	
	s 11.45 AM		s 4.13		s 8.24	400.6	401	90	67	★ HARPER	HA	DN			s 12.33	6.01		s 10.10	
			f 4.23		f 8.32	404.1	404			SWEENEYBURG					f 12.23	f 5.51			
	s 12.18 PM (4)		s 4.29		s 8.37	406.1	406	4	75	★ CIRTSVILLE					s 12.18 (65)	f 5.45		f 9.00	
	f		f 4.34		f 8.42	408.1	408	59		★ WILLIS BRANCH					f 12.13	f 5.40			
	s 12.50		4.38		s 8.44 (66)	409.1	409	15	108	★ PAX	AX	DN	W		s 12.10	5.37		s 8.44 (5)	
	s		4.42		8.47	409.9	410	54		★ LONG BRANCH					s 12.06	5.34			
	f 1.10		4.48		8.52	411.6	412	3	75	★ LIVELY					s 12.01 PM	f 5.30		f 8.05	
			4.58		9.01	414.8	415			DOTHAN					s 11.52 AM	f 5.21			
	1.25		5.04		9.07	416.8	417	71		★ SILVER GAP					11.47	5.15		7.50	
	s 1.35		s 5.10 (6)		s 9.10	417.7	418	31	81	OAK HILL JUNCTION	BS	D			f 11.43	s 5.10 (3)		s 7.45	
	f		f 5.17		f 9.16	419.9	420			LICK FORK					f 11.34	5.04			
	f		f 5.22		f 9.20	421.1	421			WRISTON					f 11.31	5.01			
	f		f 5.28		f 9.25	423.0	422	30		INGRAM BRANCH					f 11.26	4.57			
	f 2.00		5.50		9.27	423.4	423	79		★ HAMILTON					11.24	4.55		f 7.15	
5.05 P.M.-lv.	2.30 (61)		s 5.40		9.36 (61)	426.8	427			★ PAGE	D	DN	C.W. S.T.		s 11.16	4.48		7.00 A.M.-lv.	P.M. ar. 7.15
5.15	15		s 5.55		9.53	430.3	430			BEARDS JCT					s 11.05	{ 4.35 / 4.15 }		6.50	
5.20	20					430.8	431	12		ROBSON								6.45	
5.35 P.M.-ar.	35		6.15 P.M.-ar. (62)		10.12 A.M.-ar. (4)	435.3	435			DEEPWATER	VN	DN		10.50 A.M.-lv. (5-61)	4.00 P.M.-lv.	4.00 P.M.-lv.		6.25 P.M. lv. (3)	P.M. lv.
0:10	6:15	0:06	3:37	0:05	2:58					**Running Time**				0:05	3:11	3:21	0:05	8:40	0:50

RIGHT • The passenger fleet was small; from the 1920s forward just ten steel coaches, which were not air conditioned and a handful of steel head-end cars, baggage/express, baggage/RPO, etc. One notable car was #92, a 65' wooden baggage/express car built by Harlan & Hollingsworth in 1910, which survived until the merger.
(Courtesy Bob's Photo)

BELOW • The road also had at one time or another five business cars, the last three of which were based at Norfolk Terminal Station. *Winding Gulf*, named for the coal-rich branch of the same name, was built by Pullman in 1921 as the road's only steel club car. It was converted to a business car in 1938, ending all food service to Virginian passengers, and was scrapped by the N&W in 1960. *(Courtesy Bob's Photo)*

In 1920 Alco's Richmond Works delivered six 4-6-2 light Pacifics, the first of their type on the road, hence they were given the PA designation. The engines rode 69" drivers, carried a boiler pressure of 200 psi and developed 44,300 pounds of tractive effort, about the same as a PRR K-4. The engines carried relatively small tenders with 14 tons of coal and 10,500 gallons of water. The tenders had the arched rear deck typical of VGN steam power. When built they hauled heavyweight steel cars on the main line trains operating between Norfolk and Deepwater; later into Charleston via the New York Central. Other than receiving slanted front cabs as did most VGN engines, they remained essentially unchanged over their long service lives. They wore centered smokebox number boards of various designs and several had headlights that were lowered slightly from the original location atop the smokebox. Otherwise, they soldiered on remarkably unchanged until the end of passenger service in January 1956. No diesel ever pulled a passenger train on the Virginian. All six PAs were scrapped between 1957 and 1960.

ABOVE • On May 18, 1954 PA 214 rested at Sewells Point between runs. This engine carried its headlight just below the top of the boiler and wore a cast number board. *(John Pickett)*

ABOVE • This broadside shot of 213 sitting out of service at Sewells Point in September 1956 shows the balanced, graceful lines of these engines and the arched deck of the tenders. The tenders also carried big backup lights and raised water troughs. 213 also reveals the loving care East End locomotives received at Sewells Point: aluminum paint on running board edges, driver centers and Prime cylinder relief valves; and boilers wiped down with fish oil. The Laird crosshead also appears to be painted yellow-orange, which might be a form of protective coating for crossheads were typically painted aluminum. *(H. Reid, collection of D. Wallace Johnson)*

ABOVE • If this scene of #3 at Stewartsville, Virginia, behind PA 212 looks like a typical passenger train from the 1920s, well that is what nos. 3 and 4 were until the very end. But they were also beautiful! May 30, 1954.

(Homer Newlon, collection of D. Wallace Johnson)

BELOW • We leave this study of passenger operations with a shot of #4 passing Nutbush at track speed with a clear stack and an immaculate ballast line. Steam engines mandated that foliage be cleared back from the track and the annual controlled burning of rights-of-way facilitated keeping weeds, etc. away from the track. Compared to contemporary railroading, this scene reveals a level of care and attention to detail that is hard to find on the railroad scene as we write this. *(A. Thieme)*

ABOVE • The scenery and bridges between Victoria and Roanoke are spectacular, but the line is remote. Few color slides exist from this territory so we will move west to Roanoke, 243 miles from Terminal Station and at an elevation of 926 feet. The "climb" to Roanoke had a maximum grade of just 0.6% against westbound traffic; that would change west of town. Just east of Roanoke, near a power plant on the Roanoke River, was the quaintly named Buzzard Rock Ford. It seems obvious that buzzards congregated there, but why? Perhaps the ford was hazardous, or the air drafts along the river well-suited for soaring. In any event, the spot was uncommonly scenic, as revealed in this May 22, 1954, photo of Train #4 behind 212 passing alongside the blue waters of the river. *(A. Thieme)*

ABOVE • Not far behind #4 came a local freight led by MCA Class 2-8-2 #480. In 1912 VGN purchased 18 MC Class Mikados from Baldwin, engines that were somewhat larger than the MBs of 1909-10. In the early 1940s, in an effort to increase the speeds of time freights on the East End, Virginian mechanical men met with Baldwin to see what could be done with existing power. The result was five MCs rebuilt with disc drivers and light weight rods to enable higher speeds. Baldwin provided the parts and Princeton shop men did the upgrade. The five MCAs handled time freights until the BAs arrived after the war. 480 was on borrowed time; Fairbanks-Morse diesels began arriving this same year. *(A. Thieme)*

oanoke; self-proclaimed "Star City of the South", a reference to the huge illuminated star that sits atop Mill Mountain on the south edge of the city, and the "Alamo for steam" as proclaimed by *Trains* magazine in 1955. Of course, that was homage to the N&W and the fine products of Roanoke Shops that continued to work into the late 1950s. Without question N&W dominated the Roanoke railroad scene from its arrival at what was then called "Big Lick" in 1852. In addition to a huge classification yard and the famed Shops, five routes radiated out from the city center. And then there was the Virginian, which arrived in 1909 and chose a route along the Roanoke River to the south of the city center and the N&W facilities. With relatively little merchandise traffic, VGN did not need a large classification yard, nor did it need a coal classification facility. It needed a place to handle a modest amount of merchandise and to handle inspections and power swaps for trains to and from the piers at Sewells Point. And, of course, it needed engine facilities to handle both steam and electric power. While the VGN facilities were only a fraction of the scale of the N&W, they were much more accessible and the railroad folks were very friendly to visitors.

RIGHT • *Employee Time Table No. 22, of July 17, 1955, and page 1 show the Third Subdivision of the New River Division, the "West End".* (N&WHS Archives)

THE VIRGINIAN RAILWAY COMPANY

NEW RIVER DIVISION

TIME TABLE NO. 22

EFFECTIVE 12:01 A.M. SUNDAY, JULY 17, 1955

EASTERN STANDARD TIME

For the government and information of employes; not for the public.

R. W. HUNDLEY
Superintendent

B. MILLS
Asst. General Manager

D. C. KING
Vice President & General Manager

		Third Sub-Division—Roanoke to Elmore		
Station Number	Miles from Norfolk	TIME TABLE No. 22 Effective 12:01 A.M., July 17, 1955 STATIONS	WESTWARD Third Class 63 Mon.Wed.Fri. Local Freight	EASTWARD Third Class 64 Tue.Thur.Sat. Local Freight
243	243.1	★ ROANOKE	AM-L 7 45	PM-A 3 00
247	246.8	BELT LINE — N. & W. RY. CROSSING-INTERLOCKED		
251	250.9	SALEM	8 05	2 25
257	256.6	WABUN	8 20	2 09
261	260.9	KUMIS	8 30	1 59
262	262.0	LAFAYETTE		
266	266.3	IRONTO	8 45	1 45
270	269.6	FAGG	8 55	1 35
272	272.4	ELLETT	9 02	1 25
276	276.3	YELLOW SULPHUR		
278	278.3	MERRIMAC	9 20	1 04
279	279.1	SHELBY	9 25	1 02
284	284.2	PEPPER	9 36	12 50
286	287.7	★ WHITETHORNE	9 50	12 40
293	292.7	McCOY	10 25	12 25
296	296.0	GOODWINS FERRY		
298	298.2	EGGLESTON	10 40	11 35
303	303.4	PEMBROKE	10 52	11 24
306	306.5	RIPPLEMEAD		
307	307.3	KLOTZ — N. & W. RY. CROSSING-INTERLOCKED		
309	309.2	NORCROSS	11 20	11 00
315	315.1	CELCO	11 35	10 40
317	317.4	NARROWS	11 50	10 20
321	320.8	RICH CREEK	12 10	10 00
324	323.8	GLEN LYN		
326	325.8	HALES GAP		
328	327.8	KELLYSVILLE	12 45	9 35
330	329.8	OAKVALE		
335	335.2	INGLESIDE	1 28	9 15
340	340.2	PRINCETON	1 46	9 00
345	345.0	KEGLEY		
349	348.6	KING		
352	351.5	ROCK		
355	355.5	★ M. X. TOWER		
356	356.2	MATOAKA		
358	357.7	WEYANOKE		
360	359.9	CLARKS GAP		
361	361.3	ALGONQUIN		
364	363.3	MICAJAH		
366	366.4	COVEL		
368	367.8	HERNDON		
371	371.1	BUD		
372	372.0	ALPOCA		
374	373.9	TRALEE		
375	374.5	★ ELMORE	PM-A	AM-L

ABOVE • The Virginian never invested in diesel switchers; the H16s did double duty as yard and road power after dieselization. H16 #42 was switching at Roanoke on September 2, 1957, with a loaded battleship gondola first out. This broadside angle shows how impossible it was to identify a unit by number from the side of the engine.
(*William T. Clynes*)

ABOVE • The Virginian yard in Roanoke was, and still is located on the south side of the city along a beautiful crescent in the Roanoke River. Because Roanoke was the eastern end of the electrified territory, the yard was strung end-to-end with catenary. Today Norfolk Southern stages eastbound coal trains in South Yard, a continuation of the post-merger traffic pattern of loads east on the VGN, empties west on the N&W/NS. From a bridge over the west end of the yard Russell Munroe captured SB Class 0-8-0 #252 either swapping a caboose on an eastbound coal drag or getting ready to give it a kick east. The coal car immediately ahead of the cab is one of 1000 class H-8A 55-ton composite (steel with wooden sides and floors) hoppers built in the Princeton Shops in 1944. After the War and into the 1950s the wood was replaced with steel sheet. It is July 31, 1951 and the air is remarkably clear on what must be a hot and humid summer day. *(Russell F. Munroe, Jr.)*

ABOVE • Seven years later, July 1958, H16-44 33 was drilling the west end of the yard along a muddy Roanoke River. Very little has changed since 1951, other than the diesel and the plants reclaiming the river bank. The Roanoke is a rarity, a river that railroads did not choose to follow on its southeasterly course to the North Carolina coast. *(H. A. Cavanaugh)*

ABOVE • H16s 44-22 were working the west end of the yard in 1958. The 1600-horsepower units were found from Roanoke east, in every kind of service. In this view one can easily see the differences in body styles between 22, delivered in 1955, and 44, delivered in 1956. The differences are in the radiator treatment, the walkways and the fuel tanks. *(Bob Clarkson)*

BELOW • An unidentified EL-1A unit brought a work train through the yard at Roanoke in 1958. By this date, two years after the EL-C units had been delivered by General Electric, the few motor-generators still active were in local or work train service. *(Bob Clarkson)*

ABOVE • A 1948 Timken advertisement contrasted the "other" streamlined General Electric freight locomotive of the time, the 5,000 hp single-unit Great Northern machines.

RIGHT • EL-2B 127 approached the east end of the Roanoke yard with mixed freight ahead of coal on July 30, 1958. For obvious reasons the four big General Electric products were known to VGN men as the "Streamliners".

(Richard Jay Solomon)

ABOVE • Bob Clarkson chose the Jefferson Avenue overpass to shoot this coal train with 136-137 along the Roanoke River. The river looks placid in this 1958 scene, but from time to time it has flooded with disastrous results for the railroad and for the city. *(Bob Clarkson)*

BELOW • Bob returned in 1959 and found EL-C 137 sitting beside the Roanoke Motor Shed. The Shed has a high ceiling to clear the pantographs, but as a safety measure the catenary did not extend into the building. *(Bob Clarkson)*

ABOVE • There were many photographs taken in the VGN engine facility at Roanoke, but few that captured the entire scene. On July 19, 1955 George Dimond found a vantage point on the high ground above the north side of the yard to give us this view of the facilities at the east end of the yard, at the base of Mill Mountain. Sharp eyes will find steam, diesel and electrics amidst the usual clutter of turntable, roundhouse, motor barn, coaling facility, etc. In the background are the city's Victory Stadium and, beyond that, Roanoke Memorial Hospital. To the left, at the east yard throat, one would find the VGN passenger station and a crossing of the N&W's Winston-Salem line.

(George Dimond)

ABOVE • MB 429 steamed quietly beside the Roanoke roundhouse on September 13, 1953. Roanoke had a twelve stall roundhouse, a 120' through deck turntable with machine shop, a power house and stock pens. *(A. Thieme)*

LEFT • It appears that AG 903 had just been inspected or tested as it sat in the roundhouse at Roanoke in July 1959. *(Bob Clarkson)*

LEFT, CENTER • Two of the DE-S units and EL-3B 106 were being serviced in 1955. By this date most coal trains were being hauled by big GE electrics; the EL-3B "Squareheads" were in local and pusher services with occasional work on through freights. *(John Pickett)*

BELOW • On an overcast day in July 1958 two two-unit sets of EL-C electrics, new in 1956, rested next to DE-S units. These units wore a black and white version of the herald. The electrics brought trains to Roanoke from Elmore and the diesels hauled them to Sewells Point. The Virginian had a simple mission, was designed and built to the highest engineering standards to attack that mission, and delivered impressive results year after year. Its operating ratio, the ratio of operating expenses to operating revenues, a key measure of railway operating performance, was 46.6% for 1957 and 51.1% for 1958, the road's last full year. Most railroads of that era, other than the Pocahontas roads, posted operating ratios in the 90s.

(H. A. Cavanaugh)

Along with the initial order of Train Masters came six H16-44 units, sometimes referred to incorrectly as "Baby Train Masters", a name which is properly applied only to the 1600-horsepower, six-axle model, the H16-66. On the VGN they received Class DE-S, for diesel-electric switcher, nos. 10-15. More units came in 1955 and 1956, for a total of 38. The number series included a 48 and 49, two units delivered to replace wrecked units 23 and 28. Fairbanks-Morse was able to deliver 200 horsepower per opposed piston cylinder, a feat no other builder could match at the time. Thus, the Train Master was rated at 2400 HP from 12 cylinders, and the H16-44 produced 1600 HP from an 8 cylinder version. In the opposed piston engine a crankshaft at each end of a vertical engine block drove pistons towards each other to create the combustion pressure and heat necessary for a diesel to function. The engine was basically a submarine engine adapted for railroad use. While powerful, they had a tendency to leak oil and water, and their crankcase layouts made maintenance difficult. Fairbanks-Morse would not last long in the locomotive business, but its products would serve both VGN and N&W well for many years. When the 1954 orders were received, President Beale was able to report to shareholders that 44 "unserviceable" steam freight locomotives had been retired that year. They could hardly have been "unserviceable"; they were working until the diesels arrived, but his point was made.

ABOVE • DE-S 14 was at Roanoke shortly after delivery in 1954. These units were used as switchers at Roanoke, Victoria and Sewells Point, and in pairs handled time freights nos. 71/72, Roanoke/Sewells Point. The car body of the first order of H16s had a large radiator and lowered walkway on the long hood, which was the front on the VGN. The lowered walkway required a steep set of steps up the front deck to the crosswalk. (*William Ellis*)

LEFT • DE-S 25 looks as if she has just left the factory in this photo taken at Roanoke in July 1959, five months before the merger with the N&W. This view shows the early style car body very clearly. (*Bob Clarkson*)

ABOVE • Four of the 1600 HP FM units rested between runs on September 2, 1957. The Virginian circular herald was designed at Princeton in 1936 for use on the road's 1937 calendar. It found its way, in varying forms and colors, onto rolling stock, locomotives and paper materials from then on.

(William T. Clynes)

ABOVE • Bob Clarkson captured a rare interior shot of two H16s inside the Roanoke roundhouse in July 1959 in a composition that shows well the car body differences within the class on VGN. *(Bob Clarkson)*

LEFT • Those of us who enjoyed the distinctive "burble" of opposed piston power wish Fairbanks-Morse had succeeded. This is the builder's plate from an H16 built in November 1956. *(Robert J. Yanosey)*

FAIRBANKS-MORSE

F M

MANUFACTURED BY FAIRBANKS, MORSE & CO.
SERIAL NO. 16L-132 CHICAGO, ILL. U. S. A. DATE 11-1956

As steam locomotives vanished in the mid-1950s, fans turned increasingly to the N&W, one of the very few remaining pockets of steam operation. To capture the magic of steam one final time, the National Railway Historical Society brought its annual convention to Roanoke for a week in 1957. The principal focus naturally was the N&W and its operations over Blue Ridge and west to Bluefield. Although the Virginian had ceased regular steam operations with the cessation of passenger trains 3 and 4 in January 1956, and the last steam engine in service, SB 251, had dropped its fire for the last time at Princeton in June 1957, Virginian still put on quite a show for its NRHS guests. Examples of each class of VGN's active motive power, diesel and electric, were cleaned and displayed beside three stored steam locomotives: PA 212, BA 507 and AG 903. As these images will show, Virginian folks took great pride in their railroad. How else to explain freshly painted and glistening steam power that has been stored for some time!

ABOVE • This is what fans saw as they entered the engine terminal on August 31, 1957. The Virginian even spread fresh ballast as paths through its engine terminal. High up on Mill Mountain can be seen the star, illuminated at night, which gave the city its nickname. *(Lawson Hill, collection of Boston Chapter, NRHS)*

RIGHT • Class EL-3A 100 was 32 years old and still in service in 1957. It is doubtful that the engine had looked so nice since it was last shopped! Even the "Safety First" stenciling was renewed for the occasion. Notice that the units have been spotted on the steam locomotive coaling facility with pantographs extended…but without catenary. There was no need for catenary over this track. *(William Volkmer)*

LEFT • Next we see a massive EL-2B electric motor set, 126, one of four such two-unit sets delivered by General Electric in 1948. We will learn more about these units later; for now note that the beasts wore yet another version of the VGN herald, yellow on black. We note again that these units are not spotted under catenary. Perhaps that was a safety measure; perhaps it was the only way to display so many units.

(John P. Stith)

BELOW • Year-old EL-Cs 138-139 were among the final engines purchased by the VGN; twelve 3300-horsepower units delivered by General Electric in 1956. Check out the ballast line.

(Lawson Hill, collection of Boston Chapter NRHS)

ABOVE • PA Class 4-6-2 212 never looked better than this fine day, coupled to one of the road's baggage/RPO cars and a coach, a replica of Trains 3 and 4 in their heyday. Graphite smokebox, gloss black boiler, aluminum touches, and red-orange window sashes! Magnificent! *(William T. Clynes)*

BELOW • BA Class 2-8-4 507 shows a little more wear and tear from storage than 212, but she still is a picture of regal grace, steam royalty. Of course, 507 was displaced by diesels before 212 made her last run in January 1956. *(William Volkmer)*

it takes more than S·P·E·E·D

Coupled with today's need for speed is the problem of moving a large volume of traffic. The Virginian has realized this and is meeting these demands with a fleet of modern Lima-built 2-8-4's capable of moving freight at speeds closely approximating passenger schedules.

LIMA LOCOMOTIVE WORKS INCORPORATED, LIMA, OHIO

LEFT, TOP and BOTTOM, BELOW • Then there was the biggest of them all, the steam equivalent of the GE EL-2Bs, the massive AG 903. In storage for two years prior to this display, she was all dolled up for the Convention and looked better than at any day other than her birthday. *(Three photos, William T. Clynes)*

ABOVE • The following April George Dimond dropped in on the VGN engine facility and found two of the Convention subjects back on the roundhouse radial tracks with three SB 0-8-0s and an auxiliary water tank quietly awaiting the inevitable. One suspects that had the N&W merger not occurred the Virginian would have made donations of some of its steam power, but we will never know. Only SA 0-8-04 survived because it was donated to the city of Princeton before the merger. *(George Dimond)*

ABOVE and BELOW • On September 13, 1953 August Thieme visited the Virginian passenger station at the east end of the Roanoke yard and recorded Train #4 standing at the station and then accelerating out of town under Walnut Avenue, banging across the diamonds of the crossing of N&W's line to Winston-Salem. The block building is JK Tower, which controlled the interlocking plant. Walnut Avenue was the end of the Virginian's electrified territory. Hanging from the overpass is a warning sign that says "Danger Low Wire". Such signs were white with a yellow circle and a blue center, and were found throughout the electrified territory. *(Two photos, A. Thieme)*

ABOVE • The following year John Pickett captured PA 214 on Train #4 standing at the station with the customary three-car train. By the end of the year the only remaining passenger service will be nos. 3 and 4 between Roanoke and Norfolk and the trains will carry a baggage/RPO and a leased air-conditioned N&W coach to comply with an order form the State Corporation Commission of Virginia that service be "improved" for a year as a precondition to discontinuance. One thing that did not need improving was PA 214. Thirty-four years into its service life, and in the waning days of passenger service, a time when most roads would have paid little heed to maintenance or appearance, 214 is a testimonial to the approach the people of the Virginian took to their railroad. *(John E. Pickett)*

VGN OVER BLUE RIDGE

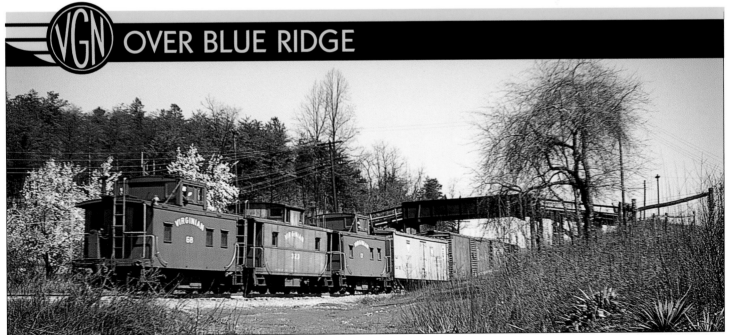

ABOVE • We will leave the East End with this image of the rear of a Virginian time freight detouring east over the N&W due to a derailment. The location is the famous "Photographers' Bridge" near Blue Ridge, crest of the eastbound climb up from Roanoke and site of so many great photos of N&W's finest power. Thieme says the train was a surprise; he was there to photograph the N&W. He also says that the train was lead by a brace of Virginian diesels, but in keeping with his policy, and that of many steam-era photographers, he refused to shoot the head end! In fact, Thieme believes he photographed just one Virginian diesel and he gave that slide away. In any event, we are forever grateful that he captured Virginian steam in its last days. *(A. Thieme)*

Roanoke was the end of the Norfolk Division and the beginning of the New River Division, the "West End" to the railroad. The Division was named for the ancient and beautiful river it followed for part of the journey west and it consisted of: the Third Subdivision, running 131 miles to Elmore, West Virginia; the Fourth Subdivision running from Elmore 60 miles north to D.B. Tower and a connection with the NYC on the north bank of the Kanawha River; and several coal branches radiating out from Elmore. It was built to tap immense quantities of very high grade, low volatile or "smokeless" bituminous coal lying beneath the mountains that separated the N&W in southern West Virginia and the C&O, which penetrated along the New and Kanawha Rivers to the north. After climbing over the mountains to enter West Virginia, the N&W and C&O snaked along river valleys and sent their coal branches up the hollows and over the ridges. The Virginian had to take a more direct, but more tortuous route through remote and rugged country to reach the valley of the Guyandot River at Elmore.

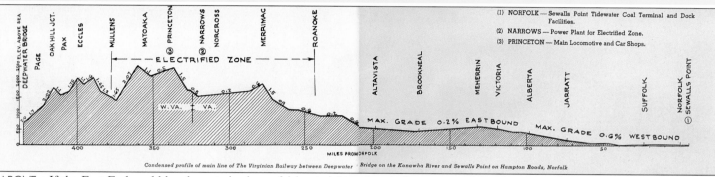

ABOVE • If the East End could be characterized as a fairly straight downhill run to Tidewater, the West End was all about curves, grades and bridges. This track profile from the 1948 Annual Report shows the challenges posed by the mountains of the West End. Rogers spared no expense in tackling the challenges of the West End; the line was built with exceptional clearances and the bridges were built to the highest loading gauge. (N&WHS Archives)

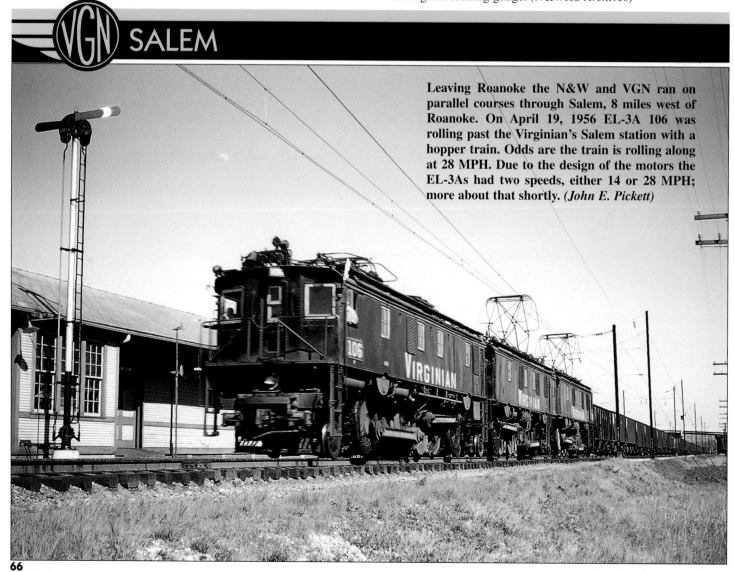

Leaving Roanoke the N&W and VGN ran on parallel courses through Salem, 8 miles west of Roanoke. On April 19, 1956 EL-3A 106 was rolling past the Virginian's Salem station with a hopper train. Odds are the train is rolling along at 28 MPH. Due to the design of the motors the EL-3As had two speeds, either 14 or 28 MPH; more about that shortly. (John E. Pickett)

RIGHT • Leaving Roanoke the VGN and N&W were roughly parallel, with the VGN climbing steadily to the south of the N&W, and both generally following the valley of the Roanoke River between Fort Lewis Mountain and Poor Mountain. At a spot called Wabun on the VGN the line crossed the Roanoke River a few hundred yards to the south of, and above the N&W crossing of the river. On March 30, 1956 EL-2B motor 126 is crossing high above the river on the deck bridge with a west-bound hopper train. *(John P. Stith)*

RIGHT • On August 31, 1957 Jim Shuman captured this view of an imposing set of Streamliners rolling across the bridge near Wabun with a loaded eastbound coal train. *(James P. Shuman)*

BELOW • Shortly after crossing the Roanoke River the Virginian turned sharply north and crossed over the N&W on one of the most unusual bridges on the railroad. August Thieme was set up to photograph the N&W on September 12, 1953 when a VGN eastbound behind a Squarehead set passed over on the skewed through truss bridge. *(A. Thieme)*

VGN KUMIS

RIGHT and BELOW • John Pickett followed the train he shot at Salem west and captured these images, the first of which was taken from the bridge carrying U.S. 460 over the railroad at the passing siding at Kumis, milepost 260.9, and the second from ground level with the bridge in the background. The train was slowing for a meet with an eastbound time freight, which enabled Mr. Pickett to get in position. At this point the N&W and VGN lines take different routes on their way to the New River Narrows, the VGN following the North Fork of the Roanoke River and the N&W the South Fork. *(John E. Pickett)*

LEFT • When the train stopped, John found the fireman surveying the beautiful Roanoke River Valley scenery. The jackshaft shows the grease of hard use. The number boards of the Squareheads were cast plates, as were the small class designation plates seen on the right edge of the photo. John recorded the images of the 106 on four consecutive frames of Kodachrome. We know he was also using black and white film, as most in that era did, because a classic photo of the meet at Kumis appears in William D. Middleton's *When the Steam Railroads Electrified*, identified as Glenvar, a nearby location on the N&W.

(John E. Pickett)

BELOW • In the same area on April 19, 1956 John Pickett also shot EL-3A #110 leaning into a curve with a westbound time freight. The Squareheads had roof-mounted jumper busses (cables) between units to distribute the 11,000 volt AC current from unit to unit, so it was not necessary for all units to raise a pantograph.

(John E. Pickett)

ABOVE • On a July 1954 day Jim Shuman caught train #4 under the catenary at Fagg, Virginia, 26.5 miles west of Roanoke in one of the lush mountain valleys of western Virginia. Most photos of nos. 3 and 4 show the same order of cars, but here we see the baggage/RPO trailing. *(James P. Shuman)*

LEFT • In an undated photo believed to have been taken near Fagg in 1956, EL-3A set 105 is eastbound with loads. Behind the set is one of the "battleship gons" rated at 105 tons. Sharp-eyed observers will note that in this age, long before unit coal trains, the big gons were indiscriminately mixed with the road's 55 and 70-ton hoppers. It mattered not, for all the coal was destined for the piers at Sewells Point equipped to unload the big cars. *(James P. Shuman)*

LEFT • After crossing the N&W the VGN began a thirty-five mile climb to the crest of the Alleghany Mountains at Merrimac, the last 7 miles of which, from Fagg to the top, was 1.5% against westbound traffic. In the early days Fagg was a base for westbound helpers. In July 1956 an EL-2B motor set was humming east through Fagg, down the 1.5% grade from Merrimac with a coal drag. Your authors have been told that despite the immense horsepower output of the big GEs, one had to be extra careful trackside because they were so quiet. *(S. Goodrick)*

The New River, despite its name, is one of the oldest rivers on earth. It is unusual in that it flows north from its headwaters in North Carolina, through western Virginia to West Virginia, where it produces deep canyons on its way to its confluence with the Kanawha River. As with all rivers during the early days of westward railroad expansion, the valleys of New River were seen as routes west. But to get to New River Valley in western Virginia, one had to surmount the first of numerous high ridges that form the Appalachian Range, running generally northeast to southwest across West Virginia and western Virginia, and on south. The N&W, as the first to arrive, reached New River via its summit at Christiansburg, then down to river level at Walton. The Virginian crossed the same ridgeline a few miles to the north, between Christiansburg and the college town of Blacksburg, at a spot it called Merrimac. The name is familiar to Civil War historians as one of the names, the other being the *Virginia*, of the Confederate ironclad boat that battled the Federal ironclad *Monitor* to a bloody draw in Hampton Roads. It has been said that the coal that fired the boat came from mines in the area of Merrimac. On the Virginian, Merrimac was at the top of a 1.5% westbound grade, and it sat under the track of N&W's Blacksburg Branch, which ran from Christiansburg to Blacksburg.

ABOVE • On May 5, 1956 a westbound extra was passing under the N&W and past the telegraph office at Merrimac as the operator gave the train a "rollby". The Squareheads' days in frontline service were numbered; GE was building the EL-Cs to be delivered later in the year. *(A. Thieme)*

ABOVE, LEFT and BELOW • Jim Shuman captured an eastbound coal train at Merrimac behind Streamliner 127 on July 18, 1956. The train must have stopped for orders for Jim was able to photograph the shiny nose of the big motor as it sat under the N&W trestle, and then go back up the bank and catch it about to enter Allegheny Tunnel. White flags were standard features of VGN trains, and on the big GEs they were metal. *(Three photos, James P. Shuman)*

RIGHT, TOP and BOTTOM • From the vantage point of the N&W bridge Jim next recorded a westbound time freight behind a Squarehead set, first exiting mile-long Allegheny Tunnel, longest on the VGN, and then passing the operator and the telegraph office…and, of course, also passing the sanitary "facilities", such as they were! As the Virginia Polytechnic Institute, a/k/a Virginia Tech, in near-by Blacksburg has grown dramatically, the area around Merrimac has gone from remote to bustling. Allegheny Tunnel now passes under U.S. 460 and a huge shopping center. *(Two photos, James P. Shuman)*

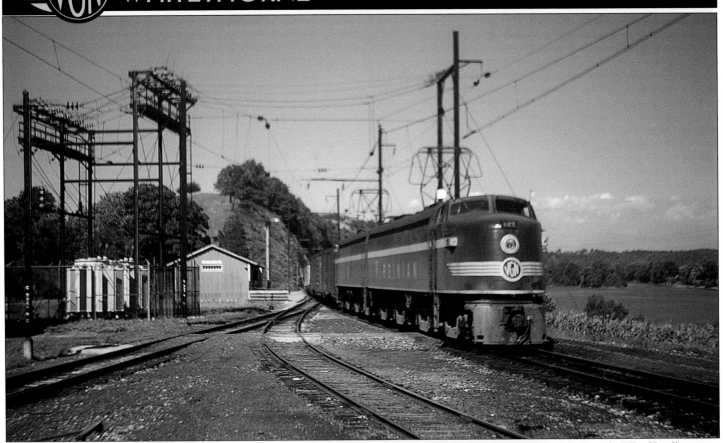

ABOVE and LEFT • Heading west from Merrimac the line dropped down 9 miles of 0.6% to reach the north bank of New River at Whitethorne, site of a power substation and a base for helpers for eastbound tonnage. While the eastbound grade was just 0.6%, it was against trains of 10,000+ tons. On August 4, 1951 at Whitethorne Jim Shuman photographed a westbound passing the orange and white station with the broad river in the background and an eastbound passing the 200-ton coaling facility no longer in use.

(Two photos, James P. Shuman)

RIGHT • From Whitethorne the line descended along the north bank of New River, passing spots that were so photogenic the railroad used them repeatedly in publicity photos. One such spot was at Eggleston, 55 miles west of Roanoke, where a rough outcropping of rock spires along the river bank, part of the New River Palisades to the south of Spruce Run Mountain, provided a dramatic counterpoint to the sleek lines of the Streamliners, as seen on the cover of the 1958 Annual Report. *(N&WHS Archives)*

BELOW • Wally Johnson stood on the N&W side of New River and captured a westbound behind a Squarehead set near Pembroke, five miles west of Eggleston, on August 11, 1956. If the scenery on the East End was unremarkable, the West End more than made up for it. The beautiful river valleys and rolling hills of Virginia led into the rugged and remote country of southern West Virginia.

(D. Wallace Johnson)

FORTY-NINTH ANNUAL REPORT

THE VIRGINIAN RAILWAY COMPANY

YEAR ENDED DECEMBER 31, 1958

"Electrified haulage of coal trains, recently inaugurated by the Virginian Railway, requires the heaviest concentration of power on a moving train ever undertaken."
Electric Railway Journal, September 4, 1926

Let us pause on our journey west and look at one of, if not the most successful heavy-duty electrified freight operations in history. Apart from the grades and the numerous mine branches, the feature that most distinguished the West End was the 133.6 mile long "Electrified Zone", as the railroad termed it, from Roanoke to Mullens. From the beginning Virginian operating men and mechanical forces had to contend with the 14-mile 2.07% eastbound climb up Great Flat Top Mountain to the summit at Algonquin and the 1.5% westbound climb from the West Virginia line to Princeton. It was the challenge of getting loaded coal trains up the eastbound grade called Clarks Gap that drove both engineering and motive power decisions for decades. In the early years the road utilized 2-8-0s, 2-6-6-0s and 2-8-2s in multiples to pull and push coal trains up Clarks Gap. As coal tonnage began to grow, the road looked for more tractive effort by experimenting first with a slim-boiler 2-8-8-2 from Baldwin that was not the answer, and in 1917 with a one-of-a-kind 2-8-8-8-4 Triplex that was huge for the time, so huge it used steam faster than the boiler could produce it! The Triplex was sent back to Baldwin and rebuilt into 2-8-8-0 #610 and one-of-a-kind Class MD 2-8-2 #410.

In 1918 Alco's Schenectady Works delivered 10 Class AE compound 2-10-10-2s for service on the West End. The engines were enormous in girth, with 48" diameter low pressure cylinders. The engines were so large that tunnel walls on Clarks Gap barely cleared the cab sides! And enginemen had to use several means to avoid suffocating in the five tunnels on the west slope. They were perhaps the ultimate in "drag" engines; the big fellas produced 176,600 pounds of tractive effort starting in simple mode and 147,200 pounds in compound, but were very slow. As a demonstration of the power of the AEs, in 1921 a single 2-10-10-2, assisted by a pusher for the climb to Merrimac, hauled a 17,050 ton coal train from Princeton to Norfolk! Of course, no one has reported just how long it took to get there. The standard operating pattern was to send "Hill Runs" of 3900-6000 tons up Clarks Gap from Elmore with a road engine from a group of USRA-designed compound 2-8-8-2s delivered in 1919-23, and two AEs pushing. A "Hill Run" would set cars off at the summit and a following train would be filled out to 8000 tons for the trip east. The operating plan worked, but it was very slow, costly and hazardous to train crews.

As coal traffic continued to grow in the 1920s, it became clear to the road that the capacity of the West End had to be improved. While it could have added more double track and worked with more steam power, the engineering, construction and labor costs would have been staggering. Instead, the road looked at the solution the N&W had undertaken starting in 1912 with plans to electrify the 2+% west slope of Elkhorn Mountain on its Pocahontas Division to the south of the Virginian. The N&W began electric operations in 1915 over a 50-mile stretch and expanded it several times as it proved to be more successful than anticipated. With that success in mind, in 1923 the Virginian Board authorized the electrification of the 133.6 miles between Mullens and Roanoke, a $15 million project awarded to Westinghouse. The operation was placed in service in 1925-26 and operated for 37 years, until the N&W discontinued it in 1962. One of the rationales for the N&W-VGN merger was to use the VGN line for eastbound tonnage and the N&W for westbound empties and other traffic. The electric operation did not suit such a one-way pattern.

The technical side of the system was a virtual copy of the N&W: the overhead delivered 11,000 volts of 25-cycle single phase alternating current (AC) to the locomotives. The overhead plant was constructed to very robust standards, in keeping with Virginian practices, so that it could carry the very heavy current loads required for tonnage operations. To meet the power demands the road built its own 40,000 KW generating plant next to New River at Narrows, Virginia, about halfway between the ends of the Electrified Zone. The plant burned pulverized coal to fire boilers that produced steam to power four 25-cycle, three-phase, 11,000-volt turbo-generators. It could burn either low-grade "bone" coal or high-grade bituminous coal or a mixture of the two. Four transformers stepped up the voltage to 88,000 volts for delivery over the catenary distribution wires to seven step-down transformers located along the line, where the voltage was stepped back down to 11,000 volts for delivery to the locomotives via the trolley wire. To assure each road a supply of current in the event of outages, the N&W and VGN constructed a connecting line between the N&W power plant at Bluestone and the VGN line. The VGN power plant was constructed with equipment sufficient to provide power to move up to 12 million tons of coal a year, at a time when the actual annual tonnage was about 7 million tons. On a daily basis the maximum load the plant could carry was 60% above the average daily load. Once again, under the direction of Chief Engineer Fernstrom, the Virginian constructed facilities that were both state-of-of-the-art and very robust.

THE SQUAREHEADS

At the time the VGN embarked on its ambitious electrification project, the N&W was operating two classes of electric motors, the second of which, Class LC-2, became the pattern for 12 three-unit motors delivered to the VGN by Alco-Westinghouse in 1925-26 as numbers 100-111. Nos. 110 and 111 were delivered as six single units so that they could be used as single units for local and switching services; the rest were semi-permanently coupled with drawbars. An onboard transformer and a phase converter stepped down the voltage

and converted the AC to three-phase direct current for two simple, but heavy-duty traction motors designed to run at one of two constant speeds, either 14 MPH or 28 MPH. Each traction motor drove a set of 62" drive wheels thru a jackshaft and connecting rods. While the EL-3As emitted the "hum" characteristic of electrics, they also had a unique slapping or clanking sound courtesy of the siderods, and from all reports their ride was fairly rough.

ABOVE • Each EL-3A unit (EL for electric; 3 for three-unit; and A for the first electric series) weighed over 212 tons and was slightly over 50 feet long. Each unit generated 92,500 pounds of tractive effort and 2375 HP at 28 MPH. Thus a three-unit set was a very powerful locomotive; one set could outperform any steam engine on the property. The first electric powered coal train out of Elmore was a 62-car drag grossing over 8000 tons and powered by an EL-3A set fore and aft. Two crews handled gross tonnage that would have taken six under previous operating patterns. In the mid-1950s motor set 106 rests in Roanoke after a run. (D. Wallace Johnson)

LEFT • Here is the "business end" of a jackshaft motor-generator unit; a traction motor at each end of the unit driving a jackshaft which was connected to 62" drivers with a main rod. 109 had been out of service at Princeton for some time by the time this photo was taken on July 29, 1958. After delivery of the EL-Cs in 1956 the Squareheads were either stored or relegated to secondary work. (Richard Jay Solomon)

ABOVE • Virginian once conducted a demonstration of the power of the Squareheads by assembling two similar coal trains at Elmore. One powered by three compound articulateds was given a fifteen minute head start up the double track of Clarks Gap, only to be overtaken half way up the hill by the electrics. When operations began, two Squareheads would take a 6000-ton Hill Run up Clarks Gap, where tonnage was filled out to 9000 tons and one EL-3A would take the train to Roanoke. Motor 101 looked fine at Roanoke in 1953. (William Ellis)

ABOVE • While the standard configuration was three units, the sets could be broken into two units or singles. They were even constructed to facilitate a four-unit configuration, but there is no evidence that they ever operated that way. On August 10, 1958 #109 appeared to be set up as two units, but it was not sitting under catenary, so perhaps it had been separated after being taken out of service. In any event, this view shows the running gear very clearly. *(Roger F. Whitt)*

BELOW • As the newer electric motors were placed in service, the Squareheads were relegated to pusher service and some were taken out of service. At Princeton in June 1960 two unidentifiable units sat beside the shop transfer table showing signs of serious scavenging. One surmises that railfans somewhere have the number boards from these units. *(H.A. Cavanaugh)*

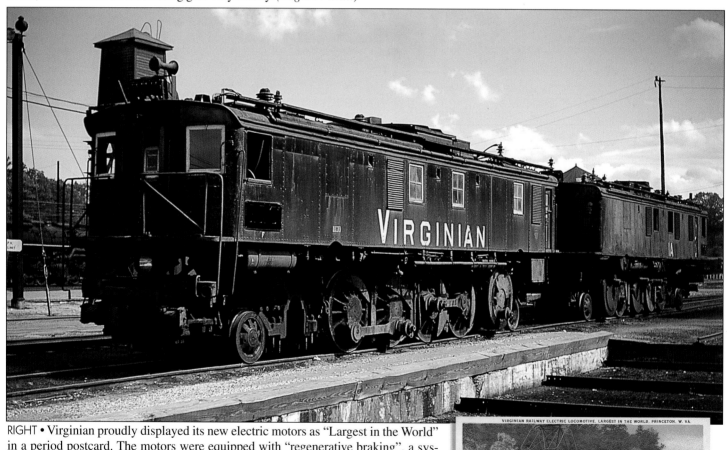

RIGHT • Virginian proudly displayed its new electric motors as "Largest in the World" in a period postcard. The motors were equipped with "regenerative braking", a system in which the traction motors were automatically converted from motors into generators when a train started downgrade thereby generating current that was fed back to the catenary. The system enabled the Squareheads to control the speed of trains on descents without using the train brakes and also generate power for the system. If there was no power demand on the system, that is, no other trains using power, the excess was dissipated at the Narrows power plant via electrodes dipped into New River. *(Collection of Kurt Reisweber)*

RIGHT • This is what a single unit, an EL-1A, looked like: #113 at Roanoke in May 1957. #113 was the last of the Squareheads of 1925-26 to operate, on a work train out of Princeton in October 1959.

(Bill McClellan, courtesy Bob's Photo)

BELOW • In 1958 EL-1A 113 was working a weed spraying train at Salem with several ancient maintenance-of-way cars. (Bob Clarkson)

ABOVE • In May 1958 class motor set 100 was about to pass a standing freight at an unrecorded location. (T. J. Donahue)

Coal traffic to Tidewater continued to grow from the 1920s forward, with only an occasional slowdown. From 7+ million tons in 1924, tonnage grew to 13 million tons by the Second World War, and was projected to continue to grow. Too, the Squareheads were beginning to show their age during the War. So in 1945 the VGN ordered four new electric motors from General Electric. In engineering and motive power the Virginian never did anything on a modest scale, and the new motors were no exception. They arrived in 1948 as streamlined semi-permanently coupled pairs stretching 150+ feet and weighing 512 tons. They were huge and they were powerful beyond anything on the railroad: 6800 horsepower, a starting tractive effort of 260,000 pounds, and a continuous tractive effort rating of 162,000 pounds. In terms of continuous tractive effort, they were the most powerful in the world. And some would say the most attractive as well.

Externally they were dramatically different from the EL-3As; they were streamlined, which gave rise to their nickname, and they were all-welded. They rode on four two-axle trucks with 42" wheels. The trucks were set up so that any truck could be substituted at any position. Traction motors were GE 746 models designed for heavy electrics and diesel-electrics. With this locomotive the historic physical and electrical distinctions between pure electrics and diesel-electrics began to blur. Each body rode two cast-steel span bolsters with two trucks under each. The two units were connected by a cast-steel drawbar through the span bolsters. The "A" units carried two pantographs and the "B" units carried one.

Internally, the differences were even more radical than the external. The EL-2Bs were derivative of the Great Northern's electric operation over the Cascade Mountains in Washington. Instead of the phase-converter system of the Squareheads, they had a motor-generator system wherein a transformer reduced the 11,000-volt AC, which was then fed to a motor which drove a pair of direct current (DC) traction generators and exciters. More simply stated, they converted high voltage AC to lower voltage DC to drive GE traction motors suspended on each axle of four two-axle trucks, a B+B+B+B arrangement in diesel-electric terms. The units had regenerative braking that produced a horsepower rating of 7800-7900 HP, enough to control downhill trains without the use of train brakes. As a sidelight, the Narrows power plant was upgraded in 1957 to increase its generating capacity to 50,000 KW as tonnage continued to grow.

RIGHT • *Here is the builder's plate from one of the EL-2B units and the version of the VGN herald applied to the sides of the "B" units.*

(James P. Shuman)

ABOVE • The Streamliners arrived in 1948 and immediately reduced running times and increased tonnage per train. One set could handle a 3000-ton train on a 1.3% grade at 35 MPH, and handle a 10,000-ton train on more level ground. Whether at rest or on the move, the big GEs were something to behold. 127 was at rest at the Motor Barn at Mullens, WV in October 1958 in a moody scene. On the Virginian, electrics were "motors"; the three-stall shop at Mullens was the "Motor Barn" and the smaller, single-track building at Roanoke was the "Motor Shed".

(Bill McClellan, courtesy Bob's Photo)

ABOVE • Motor 126 at Roanoke shows the "B" end with the VGN herald only. The EL-2Bs introduced yellow to the VGN, replacing the yellow-orange that had been standard on both steam and electrics. There has been some debate about whether the units were painted black or dark green, but it is clear from GE paint specifica-tions, photos and contemporaneous observations that they were black when new. Of course, one trip over Clarks Gap and they would have returned with that dusty look that imparts a gray-green patina to a black finish. *(Don Ball Collection)*

ABOVE • EL-2B 127, at Roanoke in 1959, showed signs that something nasty had spilled or been dropped on the unit. The trucks on these 6800-horsepower units rode on 42" wheels and were interchangeable with one other. *(Bob Clarkson)*

ABOVE • On May 31, 1955 Jim Shuman captured the imposing front end of an EL-2B in western Virginia with an east bound coal train. *(James P. Shuman)*

ABOVE • The "A" unit of EL-2B set 126 sat outside the Princeton shops, pantographs down on a track without overhead power, in beautiful morning light on July 29, 1958. The pilot was connected to the front span bolster and not to the car body. *(Richard Jay Solomon)*

> *"They suited the Virginian in almost every way but one: looks.*
> *The rectifier locomotives had the beauty of misshapen bricks."*
> H. Reid, *The Virginian Railway*, 1961

By the mid-1950s coal traffic had continued to grow and those Squareheads that remained in service were approaching thirty years of hard service. Fairbanks-Morse diesels had displaced steam on mainline trains outside the electrified territory and VGN considered replacing the electrics with diesels. It opted to continue the electric operations and ordered new motors from General Electric. Twelve radically different units arrived in 1956 and 1957, classed EL-C and numbered 130-141. Each unit was 69' 6" long, weighed 174 tons, had a starting tractive effort of 98,500 pounds, and 3300-horsepower. To facilitate both road and switching service, they were built with a road switcher body, a style which apparently did not impress Reid. Their arrival enabled the road to retire the remaining EL-3As from road service. After the N&W discontinued electric operations, the EL-Cs saw service on the New Haven, Penn Central, and Conrail.

ABOVE • The VGN usually operated the EL-Cs in two-unit sets, one of which is seen here at Princeton on July 29, 1958. They brought to the VGN yet a third form of electric traction, which was developed after the Second World War and used in New Haven passenger units built in 1955. The locomotives used a bank of twelve ignitron-rectifier tubes to convert the 11,000-volt AC from the catenary to DC, which was eventually fed to traction motors hung on the axles of C-C trucks. The trucks and traction motors were the same used in conventional diesel-electrics. In fact, there exists a black and white photo of the 131 riding on C-C trucks from a VGN Train Master while the electric's trucks were being overhauled.

(Richard Jay Solomon)

ABOVE • The Bricks were to have short service lives on the VGN. The N&W merger occurred in 1959 and N&W discontinued electric operations on June 30, 1962, on which date we see several of the units, wearing their N&W numbers, shut down at Roanoke with Mill Mountain in the background.

(John P. Stith)

LEFT • The New Haven operated the same high-voltage AC traction system used by the N&W, VGN, Great Northern and Pennsylvania. To upgrade its freight roster the NH purchased all of the ex-VGN EL-Cs from the N&W in 1963, plus spare parts, for $300,000. The 12 units had cost VGN $267,710 each seven years earlier. In September 1963 several of the units, showing the signs of a year of storage, were at the New Haven diesel shop prior to reconditioning. *(H.A. Cavanaugh)*

LEFT • The New Haven rebuilt eleven of the motors and gave them Class EF-4, nos. 300-310. VGN 130 had been purchased for parts and was rebuilt by the NH into a diesel slug for hump service. According to New Haven authority, J. W. Swanberg, the NH *"...was never able to get all the West Virginia coal dust out of the complex control gear, which caused occasional malfunctions"*. Otherwise, they were said to be extremely successful on the NH, where they were known as the "Virginians". 307 and mate were ripping through New Rochelle, New York, on April 17, 1965, with merchandise. While they were used in drag service on the VGN, they were geared for 65 MPH and no doubt used most of it on the New Haven. *(Russell F. Munroe, Jr.)*

ABOVE • For VGN fans it is hard to see these units in other than VGN black and yellow, but they do look nice in clean NH dress, kicking up dust at Signal Station 26, Rye, New York in May 1964. The units were built with an 11,000-volt bus jumper (cable) between the units so one unit could draw power from the catenary for both. The roof canopies over the walkways were to protect the crew from 11,000 volts. The box-like protrusion on the roof housed the resistors. *(Frank W. Schlegel, collection of J.W. Swanberg)*

ABOVE • Three of the EL-Cs were preserved after Conrail discontinued electric operations, one of which ended up in the Virginia Museum of Transportation in Roanoke, a few feet from the only remaining Virginian steam engine, 0-8-0 #4. History takes interesting turns; an engine from one of VGN's first orders and one from its last sit nearly side-by-side in Roanoke. EL-C 135 sits in the Museum next to the N&W mainline in this view from July 15, 1989.

(Bill McClure)

The countryside around Pembroke is rolling hills through which New River forms a wide valley. But then the river cuts through a ridgeline in a narrow defile between Wolf Creek Mountain on the south and Peters Mountain on the north, part of the Jefferson National Forest, creating the New River Narrows. VGN chose the spot, at the town of Narrows, to build the power plant for its electrified zone. Few places in Virginia equal the New River Narrows for scenic beauty.

ABOVE • The slide capturing this image has no date or location, but it appears to be the country around Rich Creek/Narrows, Virginia, in the mid-1950s. In any event, it is great action shot of an EL-3A on an eastbound coal train. It appears the 106 has recently visited a wash rack. We also note that the side rods are painted gray, no doubt to facilitate inspection and detection of cracks. *(Don Ball Collection)*

BELOW • On June 28, 1950 EL-2B 126 is hauling empty hoppers west between Celco, mile 315.1, and Narrows, mile 317.4. In the background is the huge chemical plant of Celanese Corporation, which not only gave Celco its name, but also was one of the largest shippers on the VGN. New River is to the right and the N&W main is on the hillside to the far right. *(S. Goodrick)*

ABOVE • Action photos of trains at the Narrows power plant are rare indeed. In May 1954 an EL-3A set is working a short local east at Narrows. Perhaps the train set off the cut of hoppers in the background.

(James P. Shuman)

LEFT • Approaching Glen Lyn, Virginia, months-old EL-C 140 and mate led a westbound hopper train in September 1957. The VGN catenary looks fairly delicate but in fact was heavy duty, with steel H columns spaced at 325'.

(H. A. Cavanaugh)

Rogers pushed the Deepwater Railway east to join with his rail gangs constructing the Tidewater Railway west from Sewells Point to the West Virginia line. By 1909 the names had changed to The Virginian Railway and the lines had joined at Glen Lyn, Virginia, on the boundary between Virginia and West Virginia. The line coming east from Princeton descended along the side of a ridgeline above East River on the south side of New River. The Tidewater line was on the north side of New River, and quite a bit above waterline. Thus, the line had to cross New River at Glen Lyn, which it did on a spectacular bridge 2155 feet long, whose concrete piers were the tallest in the world when completed. The bridge, yet another example of the bold approach Rogers took to building his railroad, would be forever linked to the VGN.

ABOVE and BELOW • On one of his trips to VGN country, unfortunately undated but before the end of 1955, Jim Shuman photographed Train #3 crossing the big bridge at Glen Lyn, 129 feet above the river. In the background is a power generating station owned by Appalachian Power Company.

(Two photos, James P. Shuman)

ABOVE and BELOW • In a spectacular pair of shots that capture the grandeur of the Glen Lyn Bridge and the massive size of the EL-2Bs, a westbound hopper train crossed the New River and passed over the N&W main on the south side of the river. The spur in the foreground leads into the APCO power station. The N&W mainline made a sweeping curve to the south around the power station and began its own climb up the valley of East River on its way to Bluefield.

(Two photos, James P. Shuman)

We leave Glen Lyn after another spectacular shot of an eastbound coal train passing over the N&W main behind two of the ignitron-rectifier units delivered by GE in 1956. *(Roger F. Whitt)*

From Rich Creek, three miles east of Glen Lyn, to Kellysville, four miles west of the bridge, the VGN ascended at a maximum grade of 0.8%. At Kellysville the climb began in earnest, 10.9 miles of 1.5% to reach Princeton, elevation of 2438 feet, home of the road's main shop facilities and in the early days a classification yard for eastbound coal. The climb passed through rugged country marked by ridgelines and deep valleys, which required several impressive trestles.

ABOVE • Two miles west of Glen Lyn sat a water tank at Hales Gap, West Virginia. Having ascended a grade of 0.8% from Rich Creek and facing 10.9 miles of 1.5%, the PAs on Train #3 had to top off their tanks before heading upgrade to Princeton. #3 is taking water at Hales Gap in this scene from 1955. The pop valves are lifting, indicating the rated 200 pounds of boiler pressure, all of which will be needed for the climb over Clark's Gap, and the tank is obviously full. One hopes there were more than three passengers this day, but it is not likely. *(James P. Shuman)*

ABOVE • EL-2B set 128 was working empties west on one of the trestles west of Hales Gap on July 18, 1956. *(James P. Shuman)*

ABOVE • This view of the same train, in the deep cut east of Princeton, reveals that the EL-2Bs were set up for four pantographs, but were equipped with three. The fireman no doubt has seen many a photographer at the top of this cut, a favorite location. *(James P. Shuman)*

BELOW • Jim Shuman was a big fan of electric traction, which eventually brought him to the remote scene of the Virginian electric operations: the rugged country between Mullens and Roanoke. Jim captured the Train #3 at Oakvale, West Virginia, eighty miles west of Roanoke, crossing the first of several trestles on its way to Princeton, ten miles west. The typical consist of nos. 3 and 4 until the last year of operation was a steel baggage/RPO and two steel coaches in Pullman Green with gold lettering.

(James P. Shuman)

The town of Princeton sits on a plateau south of Great Flat Top Mountain. Princeton provided the best available open space in the area on which to build shop and yard facilities, which the railroad did. The headquarters of the New River Division was established at Princeton and both a locomotive back shop and car shops were constructed. Locomotives and cars were repaired at Princeton and cabooses and thousands of hoppers were built by shop forces. In the early days coal trains were assembled at Princeton and pushers were used on eastbounds to the summit at Oney Gap Tunnel. Later, Hill Runs were assembled into road trains at the top of Clarks Gap for the run to Roanoke and operations at the Princeton yard diminished. After the N&W merger the shops were relegated first to car repair work and then to maintaining roadway equipment. Today the station and yard tracks are gone; the abandoned shop buildings remain as a ghost town of memories!

ABOVE • We are looking south (east by timetable) at the station/office building at Princeton, an imposing and impressive two-story structure painted gray with brown trim in this photo from July 6, 1953. The shop complex is to our rear. The building, similar to the one at Victoria, Virginia, housed passenger facilities and the offices of the New River Division. It sat next to the mainline and 18 yard tracks. How to explain the car sitting up on the platform?

(Arthur Angstadt, collection of Hawk Mountain Chapter, NRHS)

ABOVE • This is a very early postcard view of the station/office building at Princeton in the original orange and white paint. *(Collection of Kurt Reisweber)*

ABOVE • This great view from George Dimond not only shows the scale of the VGN shop complex, but also provides a sampling of just about everything Virginian on July 21, 1955, other than diesels! One finds electrics, steamers, work equipment, freight cars, and passenger equipment.

(George Dimond)

LEFT • Jim Shuman continued to follow Extra 128 West and recorded this view of the train entering the Princeton terminal. To the south of the station are the Railway Express Agency building and the VGN freight house. By this date, July 1956, the yard at Princeton was not used to classify eastbound coal. The hoppers are either awaiting a trip to the mines or are in town for repair work at the shop complex.

(James P. Shuman)

ABOVE • Proof that EL-3As sometimes worked as two-unit motors, here is 100 so configured in April 1958. That was very late date for Squarehead operation; it is a safe assumption that 100 was in yard or work train service. *(Roger F. Whitt)*

LEFT • At nearly all railroad shop facilities "out back" one could always find little gems. With one of his half-frame Kodachromes Reid recorded one of the Virginian's little jewels, EA Class 4-4-0 295, at Princeton in August 1952. The Deepwater Railway purchased six of these engines from Baldwin in 1906-07, a fairly late date for this type of engine, for use in passenger services. Five of the engines were scrapped in the 1930s, but the 295 was still in service until 1953. (*H. Reid, collection of A. Thieme*)

LEFT, CENTER • Here is another one of those early half-frame images from August 1952: USA Class 2-8-8-2 710 sitting at the shops in Princeton, fresh from the paint shop and sparkling. During the First World War the railroads were "federalized" under the United States Railroad Administration as a national emergency, war-time measure to assure that war materiel would flow. The USRA mechanical design committee came up with a number of standard steam locomotive and car designs, including a compound 2-8-8-2. At that time the VGN was operating six 2-8-8-2s built by Alco Richmond in 1912-13. A group of USRA-design 2-8-8-2s were assigned to the VGN and proved so successful that the road would acquire a total of 35 between 1919 and 1923. They would become the workhorses of the coal fields for decades. 710 was scrapped in 1955 after the Train Masters dieselized the West End. (*H. Reid*)

BELOW • From the early 1950s until the N&W merger, a number of steam engines were stored serviceable at the shops in Princeton; most would never run again as diesels arrived in 1954-57 to douse the fires forever. MC Class 468 was in storage at Princeton with stack capped on September 4, 1953. The 18-member MC Class, nos. 462-479, was built in 1912 by Baldwin. Their tenders carried 15 tons of coal and 12,000 gallons of water. In the background is one of the VGN's early outside braced boxcars in MOW service. (*Collection of Morning Sun Books*)

ABOVE • Among the engines stored at Princeton in 1953 was USE Class 2-8-8-2 736, looking as sharp as the day she was delivered by Alco's Schenectady Works to the N&W in 1919 as one of its Y-3 Class. She was one of a number of USRA Mallets assigned to the N&W during the government administration of the railroads during World War I. Seven of the model were sold to the Santa Fe in 1943-44 for service as helpers over Raton Pass in New Mexico, and subsequently resold to the Virginian in 1947. The VGN gave them nos. 736-742 and assigned them Class USE, for the fifth class of USRA-design 2-8-8-2s. They differed from the original VGN USRA Mallets most notably by carrying their air pumps on their right side, rather than the smokebox front, and by having a Worthington BL model feedwater heater on their left sides. The tenders were of an N&W design, not standard USRA. 736 was scrapped in June 1955.

(Arthur Angstadt,
collection Hawk Mountain Chapter, NRHS)

LEFT CENTER • Five years later, July 29, 1958, the 468 was still sitting at Princeton, showing the effects of outside inactivity. It is doubtful that she ever ran after her 1953 shopping.

(Richard Jay Solomon)

LEFT • On June 1, 1957 SB Class 0-8-0 251 was the last steam engine to operate for the Virginian. In the middle of its shift at Princeton it was taken out of service with no fanfare, no celebration, and replaced by H16-44 47. Just over a year later it sat in storage at Princeton on July 29, 1958. When the merger occurred, all remaining VGN steam engines on the property were quickly scrapped. *(Richard Jay Solomon)*

East of Princeton the Virginian had to contend, as had the N&W and C&O before it, with the series of increasingly challenging ridgelines that mark the transition from the rolling hills of the Piedmont country of central Virginia to the rugged mountains of the Appalachian Range in western Virginia and southern West Virginia. North and west of Princeton the landscape becomes high, mountainous plateaus, marked by steep slopes, deep valleys and many meandering streams and rivers. It was then, and it remains a forbidding landscape, and a paradox of beautiful vistas and unmistakable scars left by the forces of both nature and man. It was under those high plateaus that millions of years ago bituminous coal of extremely high quality was formed.

The VGN headed north out of Princeton through a gap in a ridge and then turned to the west and descended along Bluestone River 11 miles to Rock, where it had to contend with both the mountainous wilderness and the N&W and its subsidiary, the Pocahontas Land Company, which owned thousands of acres of coal lands through which the VGN had to pass. The N&W had penetrated the Bluestone region beginning in 1901 with the intention of developing the coal lands in the Bluestone drainage and also crossing over Clarks Gap into the Guyandot River Valley. By 1902 the N&W had reached Rock, named for a rock ridge through which both N&W and VGN would tunnel, and was serving many mine operations extending up the hollows from the Bluestone. By 1904 the N&W had extended its line past Rock, through Matoaka (pronounced "ma-TOE-ka") and on to the eastern base of Great Flat Top Mountain. (While we are proceeding west in our journey over the VGN, we must remember that it was built west to east as the Deepwater Railway.) Roger's Deepwater Railway was building from the north over Clarks Gap into the Bluestone region, ostensibly to connect with the N&W at Matoaka. The N&W did everything it could to stop the penetration by the VGN, including physical force, but ultimately the West Virginia Supreme Court permitted the VGN to acquire right-of-way across property of Pocahontas Land through condemnation proceedings, and the line was constructed over Clarks Gap and into Princeton. Today the VGN line over Clarks Gap remains in use by NS, although not on the scale of its heyday, but the former Bluestone Branch of the N&W, which is never more than a good stone's throw from the VGN from Rock to Matoaka, is out-of-service.

From Rock the VGN line began 10 miles of 1.25% to the top of Great Flat Top Mountain at Algonquin. Four miles west of Rock, at MX Tower, double track extended up the mountain and continued down Clarks Gap 15 miles to Elmore, milepost 374.5. Clarks Gap was a saddle at the top of the mountain through which the line passed, but the name also stood for the 10 miles of 2.07% on the west slope, against which Virginian slammed its biggest power in its daily battle with tonnage and inertia.

As we will see, the lines to the north of Elmore were also rugged, but they were lines that served many mines, funneling coal into Elmore for the trip east. The real drama was always provided by the climb out of Elmore and over to Virginia, through tiny lineside villages, many of which were "company towns", whose names have become familiar to fans of the Virginian: Tralee, Alpoca, Bud, Herndon, Covel, Garwood, Micajah, Matoaka…. Nearly all were associated with a spectacular bridge, a mine, or a geographic feature. In building his railroad through this forbidding land Rogers spared no expense; clearances were wide, track structure was robust and the bridges and viaducts were engineered for the highest live loads. On the other hand, while the physical plant was built to the highest standards, the line was unsignalled territory, governed by rule book, timetable and train orders right up to the N&W merger.

ABOVE RIGHT • *Here is the cover of employee Time Table No. 21 from August 5, 1945 for the New River Division. By that date passenger service had ended in West Virginia; only Roanoke-Princeton locals 63/64 warrant timetable space.*

ABOVE • This period postcard shows how Matoaka looked in the early days. Some of these building remain standing. (*Collection of Kurt Reisweber*)

RIGHT • Color photos of the climb up either side of Clarks Gap are very rare. The country was, and still is remote, wild and unforgiving; the few residents could be inhospitable to outsiders. It was not the sort of area one would casually hike into to get photographs. Early on the VGN had laid a second main track from Elmore over Clarks Gap to a spot called MX Tower to speed traffic over the mountain. In October 1960, eleven months after the N&W merger, EL-C 239, nee VGN 139, and two mates are bringing an eastbound coal train off double track downgrade at MX Tower. Under N&W direction the trains became longer, requiring a third unit. *(H.A. Cavanaugh)*

VGN CLARKS GAP

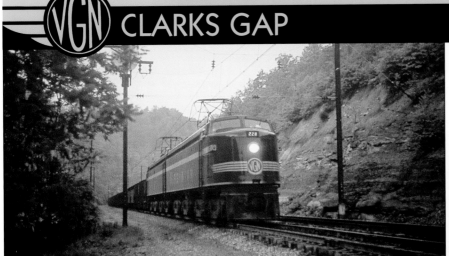

LEFT • The next eastbound was pulled by the more customary EL-2B set, in this case the 228, followed by an EL-2B pusher with an N&W steel caboose in the fastness of Great Flat Top Mountain approaching Clarks Gap tunnel. *(Two photos, Eugene L. Huddleston)*

LEFT • The August 1945 Passenger Schedule included a long list of flag stops. *(N&WHS Archives)*

THE VIRGINIAN RAILWAY

MAIN LINE between
ROANOKE, VA., and CHARLESTON, W. VA.

ABOVE • The line descends the west slope of Clarks Gap and rejoins "civilization", and West Virginia Route 10, at Garwood, site of one of the most photographed of VGN trestles. Bridge 365.4 is a 720' long curved structure with Garwood Tunnel at its east end. Squarehead 103 was leading a Hill Run over Garwood Trestle on a beautiful summer day, June 28, 1950, in a setting that can truly be called deepest Appalachia. (S. Goodrick)

VGN GARWOOD

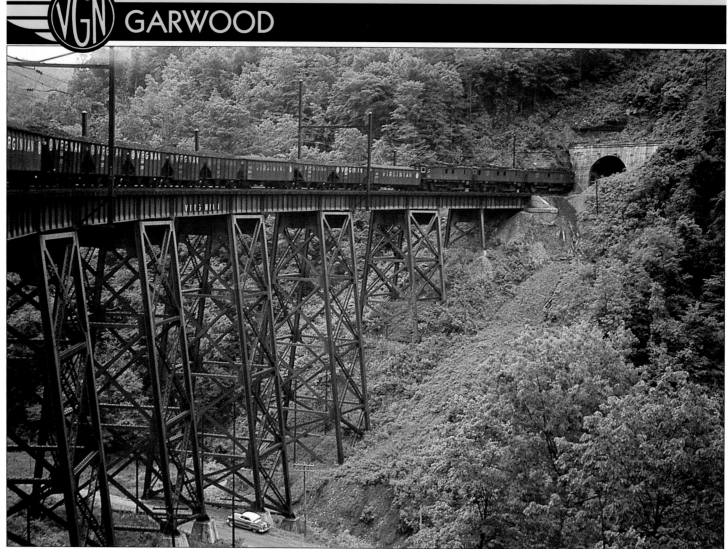

ABOVE • An eastbound Hill Run is stretched out on the 2.07% west slope about to enter Garwood Tunnel behind an EL-3A set on May 31, 1955. We can take it to the bank that there is another Squarehead or EL-2B set on the rear. Jim Shuman's snazzy two-tone Pontiac got quite a workout on the back roads of Virginian territory, and appears in several of our scenes. (James P. Shuman)

LEFT and BELOW • It must have been an adventure climbing up above the Garwood trestle, several hundred feet above the road, on a hot July 1956 day in rattlesnake country. EL-3A helper set 103 drifted downgrade, followed by a westbound empty train behind 128. It said something about the pride of Virginian folks that the railroad's name was painted high up in the air on a trestle in this remote part of West Virginia.

(Two photos, S. Goodrick)

ABOVE • One mile down WV 10 from Garwood the highway passed under another bridge featured in many photos over the years, the curved trestle at Covel, mile 366.4. On June 28, 1950 Squarehead 103 took a Hill Run upgrade at Covel at 14 MPH. At the west end of this trestle a mine spur ran along a cut in the background, above which is one of the unfortunate byproducts of deep mining, a tailing (mining waste) pile. These piles more often than not would leach bad things into the water courses, and if they became saturated by rainwater, would slide down the hollows with catastrophic results. Today there are but a handful of mines in the former VGN territory where once there had been scores, but the tailings and their scars remain. *(S. Goodrick)*

ABOVE • A year later, on July 12, 1951, the 103 was again pushing hard on the rear of a Hill Run. Beneath the bridge was the company town of Covel. Company towns were a feature of the West Virginia coal fields from the very beginning. The coal-bearing lands were isolated, rugged and often impenetrable other than by the new rail lines. The coal companies built complete towns for the miners and their families near the mine heads and charged them rent. The companies operated company-owned emporiums that sold just about everything a miner's family could need, either for "script", paper issued by the company as wages and good only in the company store, or on credit against the miners' wages, giving rise to the lyric made famous by Tennessee Ernie Ford: *"...I owe my soul to the company store."* Today many of the former company towns remain, but are municipalities of one form or another. The small "cookie cutter" homes built by the companies have taken on individual identities over the years, but they retain much of their "company town" flavor. On the other hand, the many company stores that were the focal point of life in the towns, apart from the churches, are nearly all gone other than an abandoned building here and there.

(S. Goodrick)

ABOVE • A mile and a half down WV 10 from Covel one came to the mining town of Herndon and passed under another well-documented bridge. There was once a large mine tipple at Herndon, which gave rise to the company town seen in this image from May 31, 1955. A Hill Run behind an EL-3A set was curving past the tidy little town. This is a fairly typical coal country scene: rows of small, identical homes tucked hard by the tracks, with an occasional larger home for foremen or superintendents. All in all, the life of a mine family was a daily challenge, one that shaped the character of the fine folks of this region. *(James P. Shuman)*

ABOVE • Near Herndon on July 19, 1956 EL-1A 113 is backing a work train with a fascinating mix of VGN MOW cars, including a spreader and Ditcher Crane B-24 aboard a flatcar. *(James P. Shuman)*

ABOVE and RIGHT • On June 28, 1950 the photographer set up at the Herndon Bridge and first captured a Squarehead helper set returning light to Elmore, then a Hill Run behind another EL-3A set, 103. Moving up WV 10 a short distance the Hill Run was passing one of the many tidy little white churches that could be found in and around every town. The four big GE Streamliners are two years old, but the Squareheads will continue in front-line service until the twelve EL-Cs arrive in 1956-57.

(Three photos, S. Goodrick)

ABOVE • We have finally reached Elmore Yard, milepost 374.5 from Norfolk, which sat along the east bank of Guyandot River and was the end of the Third Subdivision. (Maps will sometimes show the river spelled as "Guyandotte", but we have been using the spelling used by the Virginian in its timetables.) After leaving Herndon, then Bud and Alpoca, the main line from the east crossed Barker Creek, a tributary of the Guyandot, and passed coal mines at Deerfield and Tralee, both within the Elmore yard limits but some distance east of the yard. As it entered Elmore the main and the highway were separated by Barker Creek. On June 28, 1950 MC Class 2-8-2 468 was working the lead to the tipple at Tralee, a mine/tipple complex now gone. The Elmore power substation is in the left background.

(S. Goodrick)

BELOW • Motor set #110 was leaving the east end of Elmore with a Hill Run on June 28, 1950. *(S. Goodrick)*

ABOVE and BELOW • A westbound time freight passed with EL-2B set 127. After dropping its train in the yard, the motors have backed down to the lead to run up to the Motor Barn at Mullens, 2.2 miles north on the Fourth Subdivision. *(S. Goodrick)*

ABOVE • Gene Huddleston made several trips to the Elmore/Mullens area in the late 1950s and we are the better for it. In this scene from June 1959 we see an EL-C set returning to Elmore Yard from a Hill Run with steel caboose 339. The yard was on a fairly steep grade and curved sharply around to the north from its eastern end and followed the winding course of the Guyandot. The town of Mullens is two miles in the distance along the Guyandot and the yard tracks stretch that far.

(Eugene L. Huddleston)

LEFT, CENTER • In September 1957 Gene photographed east-bound merchandise leaving behind an EL-2B set in a scene that dramatically demonstrates the enormous size of these motors in relation to the cars behind. By the mid-1950s scheduled time freights 71/72 only ran on the East End; New River Division merchandise trains were run as extras.

(Eugene L. Huddleston)

LEFT • A Train Master with caboose 96 moved downgrade at the east end of Elmore.

(Eugene L. Huddleston)

ABOVE and BELOW • Gene returned to Elmore in June 1959 and found an EL-C pusher set about to tie onto an eastbound Hill Run; in this case it appears they must shove against the cab. While the N&W pushed on the rear of its cabs, the VGN, like the C&O, chose to place its wooden cabs behind the helpers. The VGN steel cabs had Duryea cushioned underframes and were built to the same plan as N&W versions. Thus they could withstand the compression forces of the helper units. The Bricks were long-limbed at 69' 6" in length. As the pushers awaited duty an eastbound passed behind a Streamliner. A crewman of the pusher gives the crew of the eastbound a wave as he conducts the mandatory rollby inspection at Elmore. *(Two photos, Eugene L. Huddleston)*

BELOW • The date is April 1960, just five months after the N&W merger and little has changed at Elmore. We see an EL-2B sitting across from the east end yard office awaiting duty, while the customary Train Master handles yard switching. *(Roger F. Whitt)*

ABOVE • Fast forward six months and the N&W changes are beginning. On October 14, 1960, eleven months after the merger date the EL-2B sets have had the VGN herald removed from the flanks of the "B" units and have been renumbered from the 100 series to 200. Other than the renumbering and adding a third unit to road sets, little had changed in the operations of Elmore. Here we see motor 227 ready to push a Hill Run east to the top of Clarks Gap.

(Roger F. Whitt)

ABOVE • In 1962 Jim Shuman returned to VGN country to follow his passion for electric traction, and no doubt to see what changes N&W had made to the VGN. Perhaps he knew that the wires were about to come down. In any event, this is a good view of the overall scene at the modest engine facility located at the east end of the main yard at the junction of the Third Subdivision, leading away in the background, and the Guyandot River Branch leading off to the right along the river. Before the electrification project, a roundhouse and steam servicing facilities filled this spot. At this point only minor diesel servicing took place. The Train Masters and the electric motors were cared for at the Mullens Motor Barn, two miles to the north. By the end of June 1962 the electric power will be turned off.

(James P. Shuman)

Electric Locomotive Shops, Mullens, W. Va.

LEFT • Another period postcard, this time of the Mullens Motor Barn after the electrification project was completed.

(Collection of Bill McClure)

VGN MULLENS

ABOVE • When the Elmore to Roanoke line was electrified in 1925-26, the electric servicing facilities were constructed at the town of Mullens, two miles north of Elmore alongside the Fourth Subdivision line to Deepwater Bridge. While the town was two miles north of the Elmore milepost, the yard tracks extended all the way to Mullens. The brick Motor Barn, as it was known, sat in a large wye at Gulf Junction, the point at which the Winding Gulf Branch entered the yard limits. The spot was also the confluence of Winding Gulf Creek with Guyandot River. The Winding Gulf Branch followed Winding Gulf Creek to its headwaters near Beckley, in C&O country. Jim Shuman recorded the Motor Barn scene in the mid-1950s, just after the Train Masters arrived. The four big GE motors have forced many of the EL-3As into storage. (James P. Shuman)

ABOVE • In 1960 the scene at Mullens had changed quite a bit. The N&W had sold the remaining Squareheads to Mansbach Metals in Ashland, Kentucky, for scrap value. The EL-Cs were being operated in three unit sets and at least one EL-2B set had been broken up,

with one half used in pusher service at Whitethorne, Virginia. From this vantage point on WV 16 the Fourth Sub is behind the Motor Barn, heading out to the right, and the Winding Gulf Branch is the curving track to the far left. Gulf Junction is around the curve in the

background just beyond the motor sets. We also see that the Virginian operated its Train Masters in two-unit sets with the long hood leading, a practice that was adopted by both N&W and Southern Railway. *(H.A. Cavanaugh)*

"We run some fine engines…We're continuing steam operation."
VGN President Frank D. Beale, *Trains and Travel*, December 1953

We can assume that Mr. Beale made that statement a couple of months before the *Trains* issue was published, nevertheless, we know that at the time he made it the railroad was looking seriously at diesel power for service outside the electrified zone. In June 1953 executives of the Virginian attended the annual convention of the Railway Supply Manufacturers Association for the purpose of having discussions with representatives of Fairbanks-Morse about its high-horsepower diesels.

The Virginian arrived late to the diesel party, as did neighbor N&W. The C&O began the steam-to-diesel transition in 1948, and while it tried to maintain steam operations in coal country, for obvious reasons, by 1953 diesels had replaced steam outside the Chesapeake District and had begun to come east. On the Virginian, as of the end of 1953 the average age of the most modern steam power on the road, the AGs and BAs, was 9.9 years, but the remainder of the steam freight roster, excluding switchers, had an average life of more than 35 years! Indeed, none of the latter engines was built after 1923. The 40 US-class 2-8-8-2 Mallets, which dated from 1919-23 and which were the workhorses on the mine branches, were increasingly costly to maintain. And as all the steam holdouts discovered, the supply of new replacement parts for

steam power was drying up. Then too, in the post-war years labor costs for all of American industry were rising faster than in any previous period and steam power was extremely labor-intensive.

It is no surprise then that the VGN did what all railroads would do eventually, and it is no surprise that it waited as late as it could, given its commitment to coal, both as freight and as fuel. But why did it turn to Fairbanks-Morse rather than to the more established EMD or maybe Alco? The answer is that the Virginian always had thought big when it came to power for its coal trains; big and bigger steam and the most powerful electrics built when delivered. In the early 1950s there were no single-unit freight diesels that matched the power of a single Mallet in mine run service. EMD was selling multiple-unit consists of standardized models in the 1750 horsepower range; Alco was following suit. Then Fairbanks-Morse announced the 2400-horsepower, six-axle H24-66 Train Master and sent demonstrators out from Beloit, Wisconsin, to sell the railroads.

The Virginian men that went to the convention were looking for a single unit with more than 2000 horsepower; one that would also be flexible enough to handle the sharp curves on the mine branches. Beloit sent Train Master demonstrators TM-1 and TM-2 to the VGN for a "hands on" series of tests.

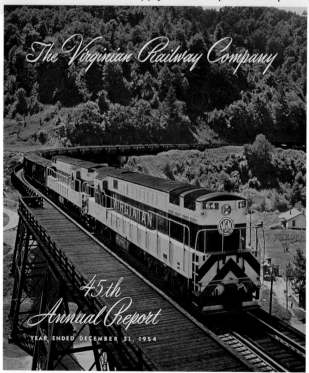

ABOVE • Unlike the N&W, which in 1955 would sneak diesels in via the backdoor of the line to Durham, VGN put them in service and proudly displayed them on the front and rear covers of the 1954 Annual Report to shareholders. VGN employee and semi-official photographer George Shands made 4x5 transparencies of the new power on the bridge at Slab Fork, on the Fourth Subdivision, for use on the Annual Report. The 64 is hauling a westbound coal train to the NYC interchange at Deepwater. For reasons which have never been explained, VGN diesels, excluding the 6, never carried unit numbers anywhere other than in the front and rear number boards. *(N&WHS Archives)*

ABOVE • Following the N&W merger on December 1, 1959, the Train Masters were renumbered by adding 100 to their numbers, but their assignments remained essentially the same, with one exception. They continued to work out of the Mullens Motor Barn in yard

They passed and in December 1953, the same month Mr. Beale was quoted in *Trains*, the VGN Board of Directors authorized the purchase of 19 Train Masters and 6 1600 HP H16-44 units for $5,305,931, the second largest order received by Fairbanks-Morse. No other builder demonstrated on the VGN, even though EMD sent F-units to both N&W and C&O. While it has been widely reported that the Train Masters were for the West End and the H16s for the East End, an interview with a former VGN manager in the mechanical department revealed that all of the original order was intended for the West End. The H16s were to switch Elmore Yard. When the VGN found out how flexible and productive the Train Masters were, it realized it did not need the H16s on the West End and they were sent to Sewells Point. When delivered in the spring of 1954 as nos. 50-68, the Train Masters enabled the road to retire 35 US-class Mallets immediately. Each US-class Mallet generated 101,300 pounds of tractive effort and each Train Master produced 98,625 pounds, making them essentially the same, and the latter was more flexible and productive. Thus, it took fewer of them to dieselize the West End than the road anticipated. It must have been quite a shock to the folks of the mountain country when the new diesels appeared in a flashy yellow and black body with imitation gold "Virginian" in 24" letters and a red and white herald on each end!

ABOVE • A pair of Train Masters was working hard on the grade to Clarks Gap with an eastbound in June of 1959.

(Eugene L. Huddleston)

service at Elmore, on the many mine runs, and also over the road to Roanoke. Slowly they were repainted into N&W black with first the script N&W herald, and later the "half-moon" version. Some would later receive the so-called "Pevler Blue" scheme that came in after the N&W acquired the NKP and Wabash in 1964 and Herman Pevler, formerly of the Wabash, became N&W President. In June 1962 a single Train Master was working hard to move an eastbound coal train over the New River at Glen Lyn. *(James P. Shuman)*

ABOVE • Color photos taken between Elmore and Deepwater on the Fourth Subdivision of the New River Division are very rare indeed. The country was remote and the line was a challenge to photograph. Leave it to famed steam era photographer Bob Collins to find his way to tiny Cirtsville, West Virginia, on a beautiful May 17, 1951 to record PA 213 on Train #4. Cirtsville was 32 miles north (west by timetable) of Elmore, between the grades of Jenny Gap to the south and Silver Gap to the north. By 1955 passenger service in West Virginia was down to a roundtrip between Page and the eastern West Virginia state line, which was mandated by the state as a prelude to outright discontinuance.

(Robert F. Collins, Morning Sun Books Collection)

ABOVE • The branches north and west of Elmore provided the stream of coal that flowed to Tidewater. A typical mine scene shows the operation of the Eastern Gas & Fuel's Kopperston Operation on the Morri Branch, off the Guyandot River line, in April 1960. For many years the Virginian was controlled by the Mellon family of Pittsburgh through its control of Koppers United Company. The actual shareholder was a Kopper's subsidiary, Eastern Gas and Fuel Associates, which not only owned vast coal reserves served by the VGN, but also was the largest shipper of coal to New England via coastal ships. It's only the year after the N&W merger, but the mix of hoppers shows the influence of the larger road, whose hoppers seem to outnumber those of the former VGN.

(Collection of Kurt Reisweber)

The Virginian Railway was merged into the Norfolk & Western on December 1, 1959. It was an acquisition, not a merger of equals, and the Virginian name disappeared from the roster of American railroads. Some changes were made quickly, while others took years before materializing. Since this is a book on the Virginian Railway, we do not intend to cover the post-merger years along the former Virginian lines comprehensively. Our coverage concentrates on the Virginian locomotives that continued to serve their new owner well into the 1970s, the fleet of Fairbanks-Morse Train Masters and H16-44s. Although the N&W was still operating some steam in 1959, it was on the path to total dieselization, which it achieved in 1960 (not counting the electric operations on the former Virginian, which lasted until 1962, as we have seen). Although the N&W had not ordered any diesels from Fairbanks-Morse, it was not about to junk the almost-new VGN FM units, the oldest of which was only five years old at the time of the merger. The Virginian engines were joined by FM units from other roads acquired by N&W in the 1960s: Nickel Plate, Wabash, Pittsburgh & West Virginia, and Akron, Canton & Youngstown. In the short section that follows, we take a brief look at FM units of VGN origin in the N&W era, and then finish the book with a look at rolling stock operated by the Virginian.

ABOVE • By the early 1970s it was clear that the remaining VGN Train Masters were going to be retired sooner rather than later. They were approaching twenty years of hard service and their builder had exited the locomotive business. Fans began to seek out the last few still in service, which led them to the tiny town of Oak Hill, 1.6 miles up the White Oak Branch from Oak Hill Junction on the Fourth Subdivision north of Elmore. Two mine branches extended out of Oak Hill on very steep grades. A Train Master was based at Oak Hill to work the mine tipples. The last in use was 171, seen here with a work train in October 1972. *(Jeremy F. Plant)*

Management of the N&W had always been sensitive to the interests of the railroad community in history and heritage, and the road had facilitated fan trips over the years in celebration of one thing or another. In November 1973 it ran a memorable trip from Roanoke to Elmore and return with two of the last five active Train Masters, nos. 173 and 174. The weather was awful, but the faithful turned out in force, both on the train and chasing it. We are pleased to present this gallery of images from those trips.

ABOVE • The special is eastbound out of Elmore. The 173 would be the last Train Master on the roster. The day after working a fan trip with the N&W's Centennial unit, SD-45 1776, on July 4, 1976, the unit was stored and then retired in September 1976, ending a colorful era.

(Jeremy F. Plant)

LEFT • 1955 FM advertisement.

RIGHT, ABOVE • It's a cold morning and the big boys have been sitting at idle for awhile. Now they send carbon aloft leaving the former N&W station in Roanoke westbound. *(Jeremy F. Plant)*

RIGHT, BELOW • Earlier in this volume we presented a photo taken from above the trestle at Garwood. Matt Herson captured the Train Master special from near the same spot during a photo run by. The train is a mix of N&W equipment and other cars that were veterans of the Southern's steam program. Compare this shot with the classic image of Squareheads on the top of page 101. *(Matthew J. Herson, Jr.)*

ABOVE • In 1967 five former Virginian Train Masters were traded to Alco by N&W against an order for five Century 630 models, which were delivered with the trucks of the traded-in units. At the mine tipple at Tralee, just east of Elmore, C-630 1137, riding on Train Master trucks, and a conventional mate are heading west in November 1973. Seven Train Masters were traded to EMD in 1969-70 against an order for SD-45s, but the trucks were not used under the new units. *(Jeremy F. Plant)*

ABOVE • Beginning in 1971 and continuing through 1981, fourteen former VGN Train Masters and six of Wabash origin were rebuilt at Roanoke Shops into Class RP-F6 Slugs nos. 9900-9919. The frames, trucks and traction motors were retained, and new bodies were fabricated. The slugs were mated with EMD SD-40s and Alco C-630s for use as heavy duty switchers. On September 3, 1977 the 1137-9907 set was working the eastbound departure yard at Roanoke. 9907 was converted in October 1974 from former N&W 172, nee VGN 72. At least the Train Master trucks survived. *(Bill McClure)*

ABOVE • Just as the Train Masters soldiered on for many years after the merger, so too did the ex-VGN H16-44 units find a home just miles from their former Sewells Point home at the N&W's huge Lamberts Point complex, where they performed all sorts of work for years. In fact, Lamberts Point became a home for Fairbanks-Morse units from other roads absorbed by the N&W, excluding the Train Masters of VGN and Wabash. The 148 rested inside the N&W roundhouse at Lamberts Point in June 1969. The unit wears a faded coat of the blue scheme that N&W adopted in 1965, which came to be called, unofficially, "Pevler Blue" after N&W President Herman Pevler, the former President of the Wabash, a road that favored blue paint for its engines prior to the N&W takeover in 1964. (Robert J. Yanosey)

ABOVE • The H16s could get down and dig, perfect for slow-speed hump service. On August 2, 1974 135-148-141 prepared to pull a cut of coal over the hump at Lamberts Point. The units will then push it slowly back through the retarders. The work at Lamberts Point was hard and the environment difficult; corrosive coal dust was everywhere and the salt air added to the corrosion, as seen in the ragged paint of units stationed there. Units based there generally were serving out their useful lives, received little in the way of cosmetic maintenance, and consequently looked worn-out most of the time.

(Bill McClure)

LEFT • In August 1969 #129, wearing the original N&W paint scheme, was heading east over the Elizabeth River on former VGN track with local freight. (Robert J. Yanosey)

This is an appropriate point to sample some of the rolling stock that passed through the shops at Princeton in one way or another. At the end of 1954 the VGN owned 16 passenger cars: 10 coaches, 1 baggage/express car, and 5 baggage/mail cars. The revenue freight car fleet consisted of 428 boxcars in four classes, 6 flatcars, 40 pulpwood racks, 2 covered hoppers, 1838 gondolas (most of which were used in coal service), and…12,394 coal cars in 9 classes. The caboose roster numbered 97 in three classes. Other than the obvious need for coal cars, VGN owned the few cars that enabled it to provide service to the relatively few on-line originators of merchandise, such as brick plants, pulpwood yards, etc. As yet no one has explained the presence of the two covered hoppers. Other than of coal cars, photos of VGN equipment of any kind are rare, and in-service photos of the two covered hoppers are non-existent at this writing. Color photos of VGN equipment are extremely rare, so we are pleased to be able to present this sampling to add to the published story of the railroad.

ABOVE and BELOW • Coach 206, seen at Roanoke, was one of the ten steel coaches in Class CH-4 built by Pullman in 1921. They were 81 feet long, carried 90 passengers and were not air conditioned. They operated until the end of passenger service in 1956. 53 was one of four Class BM-3 baggage/RPO cars built in 1921 by Pullman and used on Trains 3 and 4 until the end of service. As seen in this volume, until 1955, when the N&W coach was leased, the standard consist of Trains 3 and 4 was a baggage/RPO and two of the ten coaches.

(Two photos, Lawson Hill, collection of Boston Chapter, NRHS)

RIGHT • Car 90284, shown in maintenance-of-way gray with black lettering at Roanoke in August 1957, had an interesting history. The car was built by Pullman and purchased second-hand by the Virginian in 1917. It was converted to a business car, the only member of Class BU-2, and given the name *New River*. In 1955 it was converted to MOW service and renumbered. Behind the 90284 is a MOW bunk car or commissary car converted from a wood boxcar and painted MOW gray with a brown eave around the roof. *(Lawson Hill, collection of Boston Chapter, NRHS)*

ABOVE • One of VGN's 40 pulpwood racks was at the N&W yard at Crewe, Virginia in 1981, still wearing VGN paint. *(Bill McClure)*

RIGHT • Here is a diagram for cars in the G-4C Class which shows 760 remaining in February 1954.

(Collection of Bill McClure)

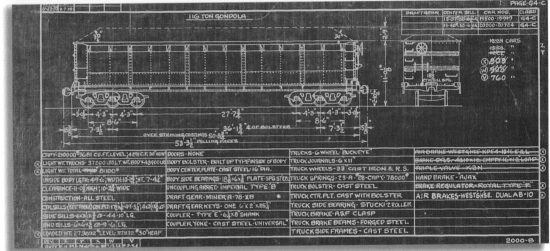

ABOVE • No piece of equipment says "Virginian" more than the famed "battleship gons". In its early years the VGN sought ways to move more tonnage with fewer cars. After experimenting with four 120-ton flat bottom gondolas in 1916-17, the VGN had Pressed Steel Car Company build 2025 similar 116-ton (later reduced to 105 tons) cars in the period 1920-24. The cars rode on either Buckeye or ASF six-wheel trucks. The original cars had distinctive fish belly sides, but when rebuilt in 1937-38 they emerged with the straight side sills seen in this photo taken at Roanoke in 1957. Since the big cars were suitable only for rotary dumping, it had been hoped that they could be used to backhaul iron ore to the Great Lakes. That did not materialize; they spent their lives running from the mines to Sewells Point. 20664 was a class G-4C built in 1924. On the date of the N&W merger 240 remained on the roster.

(Lawson Hill, collection of Boston Chapter, NRHS)

123

ABOVE • At the end of 1954 the largest single class of VGN coal cars was the 3019 Class H-6 55-ton twin hoppers built by Virginia Iron & Bridge of Roanoke between 1928 and 1931. On August 10, 1971 loaded H-6 #11536 was on the N&W at Portlock Yard, Chesapeake, Virginia, looking essentially unchanged from its VGN days.

(Bill McClure)

BELOW • Between 1947 and 1952 VGN built or purchased 4000 55-ton twin hoppers in two classes, H-12 and H-13, to essentially a single design. They were the backbone of the modern fleet until the 70-ton cars came in the 1950s and 3937 were in service at the merger date. #29265, at Norfolk on August 7, 1972, was built in 1949 as a member of Class H-13C. *(Bill McClure)*

BELOW • The final VGN design for coal cars was the H-14 70-ton triple hopper constructed at Princeton in the mid-1950s. The cars were 41' long and had a lower side sheet arrangement that was unique to the VGN. At the merger date 3299 of the H-14s were in service. 2056 is at Norfolk on July 13, 1978. *(Bill McClure)*

VGN CABOOSES

The Virginian owned three cabooses that were originally built for the Deepwater Railway in 1905-06. They were later converted to MOW service. Putting those aside, the road caboose fleet consisted of essentially two designs: two classes of short wooden cabs with high cupolas built to one plan, and a single class of steel cars that followed an N&W design. Classes C-1 and C-2 were constructed from 1909 to 1924 and numbered 7-86, 95-100 and 400-412. Nos. 410-412 were rebuilt from earlier cars. The first cars, nos. 7-76, were built by American Car & Foundry, but beginning in 1917 the shops at Princeton constructed ten cars on the frames of older wrecked C-1s, followed in 1924 by 16 new cars. The C-1s and C-2s rode archbar trucks until the end, although at least one was photographed with Andrews trucks.

In 1948-49 St. Louis Car Company delivered 25 steel cars, class C-10 nos. 300-324, that were near duplicates of N&W's Class C-2 cabs also built by St. Louis Car in 1949. From 1957 until the merger date VGN built 25 more steel cabs, Class C-10A, nos. 325-349, at Princeton from kits purchased from St. Louis Car. These 50 cabs were VGN's only modern cabs. They had Duryea cushioned underframes and rode Barber-Bettendorf swing-motion trucks. After the merger they became N&W Classes C-30 and C-30A, nos. 530300-530349, and served for many years in various N&W/NS paint schemes.

RIGHT • C-1 #12 at Roanoke in July 1953. Note the raised number, a feature which appeared on some cabs in no particular pattern. *(Arthur Angstadt, Hawk Mountain Chapter, NRHS)*

BELOW • No. 33, a C-1 built 1909-10 by AC&F, at Sewells Point on January 22, 1956. *(D. Wallace Johnson)*

BELOW • C-2 #70, built by AC&F in 1912-13, was at Sewells Point in April 1959. *(H. Reid)*

BELOW • C-1 #401, built at Princeton in 1924, was at Suffolk on April 13, 1958. *(H. Reid)*

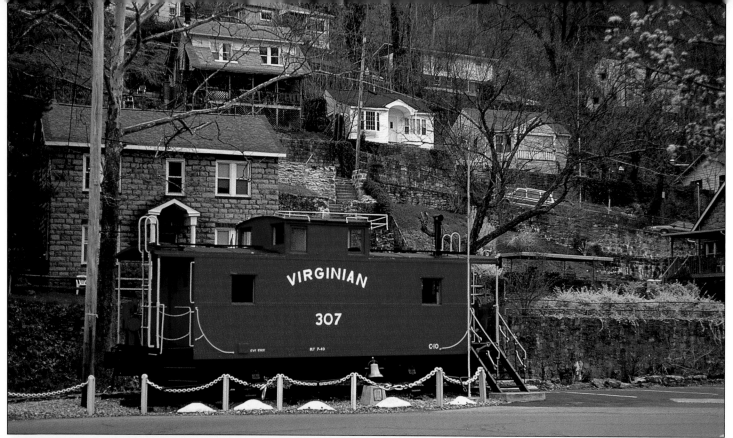

ABOVE • A number of former VGN C-10/10A cabs are in private hands, but none are tended with as much care as the 307 on display at Mullens, seen in this photo from March 2003 after the cab was restored by fans and former VGN employees following a devastating flood. *(Bill McClure)*

LEFT and BELOW • Princeton shops converted many a car to MOW service over the years, including a number of C-1/2 cabs. Here is former C-1 #2, built in 1909, sitting with a line of MOW cars at Adkins, Virginia, on the N&W's line to Bristol, Tennessee, in 1964. These cars were purchased by an individual with plans to start a tourist line, but they sat for years and nothing came of the plans. Their ultimate disposition is not known by your authors.

(Two photos, A. Thieme)

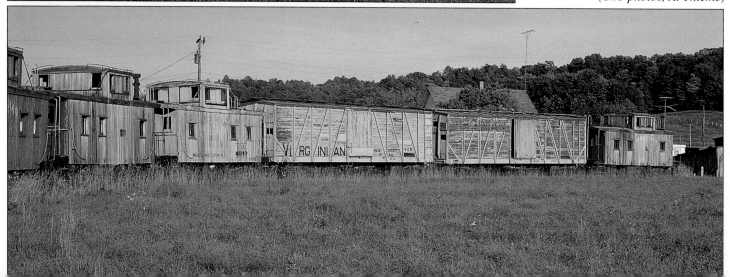

ABOVE • On March 7, 1957, H. Reid captured a former C-1/2 in MOW dress as 90187 at Suffolk. *(H. Reid)*

ABOVE • A work train with EL-1A 113 and steam powered Ditching Crane B-24, built by American Hoist & Derrick in July 1923, was leaving Princeton in September 1957. The end of the boom carried a 9/16 cubic yard shovel and, more importantly, a trolley insulator to protect against 11,000 volts! *(Collection of Morning Sun Books)*

VGN FAREWELL

We complete this volume with an enduring image of The Virginian Railway: black and yellow Fairbanks-Morse diesel, red herald, big steel and deep granite ballast. Day in and day out for fifty years the railroad implemented the vision of Col. William Page and Henry Huttleston Rogers with relentless efficiency, but also with a sense of "family" and with a style all its own.

(Steve Bogen)